T0184995

# Beginning 3D Game Assets Development Pipeline

## Learn to Integrate from Maya to Unity

**Nova Villanueva**

Apress®

*Beginning 3D Game Assets Development Pipeline: Learn to Integrate from Maya to Unity*

Nova Villanueva
Brooklyn, NY, USA

ISBN-13 (pbk): 978-1-4842-7195-7
https://doi.org/10.1007/978-1-4842-7196-4

ISBN-13 (electronic): 978-1-4842-7196-4

Copyright © 2022 by Nova Villanueva

This work is subject to copyright. All rights are reserved by the Publisher, whether the whole or part of the material is concerned, specifically the rights of translation, reprinting, reuse of illustrations, recitation, broadcasting, reproduction on microfilms or in any other physical way, and transmission or information storage and retrieval, electronic adaptation, computer software, or by similar or dissimilar methodology now known or hereafter developed.

Trademarked names, logos, and images may appear in this book. Rather than use a trademark symbol with every occurrence of a trademarked name, logo, or image we use the names, logos, and images only in an editorial fashion and to the benefit of the trademark owner, with no intention of infringement of the trademark.

The use in this publication of trade names, trademarks, service marks, and similar terms, even if they are not identified as such, is not to be taken as an expression of opinion as to whether or not they are subject to proprietary rights.

While the advice and information in this book are believed to be true and accurate at the date of publication, neither the authors nor the editors nor the publisher can accept any legal responsibility for any errors or omissions that may be made. The publisher makes no warranty, express or implied, with respect to the material contained herein.

Managing Director, Apress Media LLC: Welmoed Spahr
Acquisitions Editor: Spandana Chatterjee
Development Editor: Laura Berendson
Coordinating Editor: Divya Modi
Copyeditor: Kezia Endsley

Cover designed by eStudioCalamar

Cover image designed by - Nova Villanueva and Natalie Asport

Distributed to the book trade worldwide by Springer Science+Business Media New York, 1 New York Plaza, Suite 4600, New York, NY 10004-1562, USA. Phone 1-800-SPRINGER, fax (201) 348-4505, e-mail orders-ny@springer-sbm.com, or visit www.springeronline.com. Apress Media, LLC is a California LLC and the sole member (owner) is Springer Science + Business Media Finance Inc (SSBM Finance Inc). SSBM Finance Inc is a **Delaware** corporation.

For information on translations, please e-mail booktranslations@springernature.com; for reprint, paperback, or audio rights, please e-mail bookpermissions@springernature.com.

Apress titles may be purchased in bulk for academic, corporate, or promotional use. eBook versions and licenses are also available for most titles. For more information, reference our Print and eBook Bulk Sales web page at http://www.apress.com/bulk-sales.

Any source code or other supplementary material referenced by the author in this book is available to readers on GitHub via the book's product page, located at www.apress.com/978-1-4842-7195-7. For more detailed information, please visit http://www.apress.com/source-code.

Printed on acid-free paper

*Dedicado a mi abuela.*
*Dedicated to my grandma.*

# Table of Contents

# About the Author

**Nova Villanueva** is a professor of game design at the Pratt Institute in New York. She has taught game development for more than five years at Pratt, Parsons, and New York's College of Technology, and is an independent game developer working on *The Mills* game. She live streams her game development process at `twitch.tv/novavillan`. Nova previously worked as a 3D artist for Animatic Media, as a 2D artist for the Webby award-winning *Mafia Wars* game developed by Zynga, and is a published artist featured in *Photoshop Creative* magazine.

She has an MFA in game design from the NYU Game Center in New York and a BS in media arts and animation from the Art Institute of Fort Lauderdale, Florida. You can visit her website at `novavillanueva.com` to learn more about her work.

# About the Contributor

**Natalie Asport** worked as a 3D environment artist, character artist, medical artist, and as a hard surface artist creating vehicles and weapons for AAA video game titles such as *Just Cause 3, Just Cause 4,* and *RAGE 2*. In addition to her real-world game industry experience, Natalie earned her bachelor's degree in Computer Science from Full Sail University in Orlando, Florida.

Currently, she works as a vehicles and weapons artist at Avalanche Studios in New York. She also teaches 3D modeling for games at the NYU Game Center.

You can visit her website at natalieasport.com to learn more about her work.

Natalie Asport started working on the book as a technical editor; however, she took on work that was beyond that of a reviewer and became a second voice for this book. She has been a great contributing author to this book and is a major reason for the book being available in its present form.

# Acknowledgments

I'm eternally grateful to Natalie Asport, an AAA 3D artist and NYU professor. Without her joining me to finish this book, it wouldn't have been completed until 2077. Her second voice was what this book needed.

Secondly, special thanks to my long-time supportive friend Flo.

To Frank Lantz, Naomi Clark, Eric Zimmerman, and Bennett Foddy, professors at the NYU Game Center, who enriched my game-design process with iterative design thinking tools while I was a graduate student there. These legendary four colleagues have inspired me and will continue to do so.

This book was completely written through the pandemic, so I also need to thank my doctor, Dr.Oksana Levieva. She treated me even when regular doctor visits outside of COVID symptoms were sparse, which I greatly appreciate.

Lastly, I want to thank Delano Athias, an instructor at Pluralsight, who taught me over a decade topics from rigging to Unity. Back then, the company was called Digital Tutors and I bought their CDs. Delano taught me to see beyond memorizing tutorials and taught me in-depth tools that I can utilize to create anything.

# Introduction

You look around into a vast open space. It is hard to see through the dense blanket of fog. Suddenly, a loud thump startles you. The noise gets louder as *something* approaches, closer and closer. A large yellow mech appears in the near distance. As it walks closer to you, you start to see that it is covered in scratches, perhaps battle scars, and various signs of wear and tear appear along its edges. Its long, dark shadow looms over you. You press Escape.

Then, you go and press Play again and look around into a vast open space. It is hard to see through the dense blanket of fog. Silence lingers. A large yellow mech appears in the near distance. As it walks closer, you notice its operation buttons are distorted and its scratches and edge wear are misaligned. It is unclear what material it is even made out of. However, its long dark shadow begins to loom over you. You press Escape.

You press Play again and look around into a vast open space. This time the air is crisp and clear. A large gray mech appears in the distance. It walks in your direction. Its long, dark shadow looms over you. You press Escape.

You press Play again and look around into a vast open space. A small, default game engine character model appears in the distance. It looks as though it is walking in place. Its walking programming is not yet complete. You press Escape.

Now you are back to square one. Where it all began. An idea, a concept, a dream.

With a computer in front of you, a mouse, and a keyboard, you set out to embark on a journey. A journey where you take the tools in your arsenal and learn to build the worlds and characters you imagine, where others can play and experience. For example, a mech roaming through a post-apocalyptic wasteland.

In this scenario, the tools are the skills you'll acquire in this book as well as the literal hardware and 3D software tools themselves! Use this book as a guide to help you gain an understanding of industry standard 3D programs. The book will teach you how to create these virtual stories in a production environment.

Maya, Substance 3D Painter, and Unity are massive programs that can take years to master. However, if you keep focused on unleashing your creative self first, the rest will follow. It is not about being an expert designer, nor reaching that alluring master status. Rather, it is about being open to learning, growing, and evolving with software, technology, and your passion for the craft. This will truly help you expand your skillset as a successful 3D artist.

# CHAPTER 1

# What Is the 3D Production Pipeline and Why Is It Important?

Almost every industry is adopting/implementing three-dimensional (3D) technology as part of their production process. The 3D pipeline is the process of taking a concept through different stages of iteration, from first 3D realization in the prototype phase, to final in-game integration. These stages are composed of individual steps, such as modeling, UV mapping, setting up the overall asset for future stages in the pipeline, texturing, rigging, and bringing the asset to life.

An experienced 3D artist can see each part of the 3D production pipeline as pieces that fit together to complete an entire puzzle (an asset for a game/or how an asset fits in it). In this book, I introduce each piece as a fundamental concept and then explain how it connects to the other pieces.

In this chapter, I introduce the different types of work done by 3D artists, how they are created using different tools, and what you need to know about the 3D pipeline.

## Who This Book Is Intended For

The book is intended for novice to intermediate game developers and artists interested in understanding the 3D development pipeline of game assets. This book does not go in-depth into each phase of creating 3D assets, but helps readers understand how they are tied together as a whole.

© Nova Villanueva 2022
N. Villanueva, *Beginning 3D Game Assets Development Pipeline*,
https://doi.org/10.1007/978-1-4842-7196-4_1

# About the 3D Pipeline and How It Fits in the Game Design Process

In game development—which is a process of making a game from concept to completion—the production stage is iterative. The game's design can continuously evolve, and things that sounded great in theory may not work so well after a playtest is conducted as shown in Figure 1-1. Therefore, the development pipeline is not necessarily a linear process.

> *This prototype is played, evaluated, adjusted, and played again, allowing the designer or design team to base decisions on the successive iterations or versions of the game. Iterative design is a cyclic process that alternates between prototyping, playtesting, evaluation, and refinement.*

> —Katie Salen and Eric Zimmerman, *Rules of Play*[1]

As Salen and Zimmerman state, the work you do can be sent to quality assurance, creative or director approvals, and can often be sent back for revisions. For these reasons, a pipeline should account for revisions and course changes.

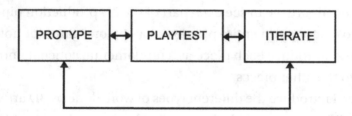

***Figure 1-1.*** *An iterative game design process flowchart*

However, when it comes to 3D asset development, there are specific tasks that have to be completed before others and some tasks that can be performed at any time. These tasks are covered throughout this book so you can understand how to work effectively. I discuss the constraints that you need to know about in order to be as productive as possible.

---

[1] Salen, Katie, and Eric Zimmerman. *Rules of Play: Game Design Fundamentals.* The MIT Press, 2010.

Furthermore, game development revolves around the following three stages: *pre-production,* which is usually a concept and an initial prototype; *production,* from a first playable game to the beta; and *post-production,* which brings the game to a master golden final build. The 3D asset development pipeline is found in the production stage.

Before I tell you more about the 3D asset development pipeline, I need to clarify the terms *3D modeling, texturing, rigging,* and *animation.* As you may have heard, these terms describe the different types of work done by 3D artists.

## 3D Modeling

3D modeling is the creation of three-dimensional computer-generated images using a digital application as a medium that represents objects in 3D space. Regardless of which 3D modeling program you use (such as Maya, 3ds Max, or Blender), the techniques and tools are similar.

A 3D artist creates 3D models that usually fall into two categories: hard surface (Figure 1-2) and organic (Figure 1-3).

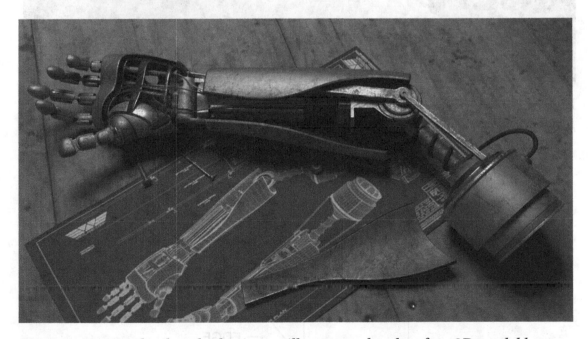

***Figure 1-2.*** *3D robot hand. This image illustrates a hard surface 3D model by Marcus Kennedy. Reproduced with permission*

Organic models are usually living things that include people, creatures, nature, and animals. Hard surface models are geometric or are mechanical in nature and include vehicles, weapons, and props. Figures 1-4 and 1-5 illustrate the fundamental process of 3D modeling, which involves the transformation of vertex points, edges, and faces in 3D space.

**Figure 1-3.**  *3D organic surface model by Michael Balzano. Reproduced with permission*

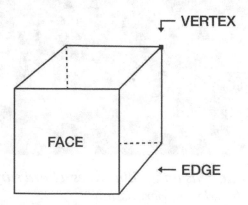

**Figure 1-4.**  *3D cube diagram showing the location of vertex, face, and edge*

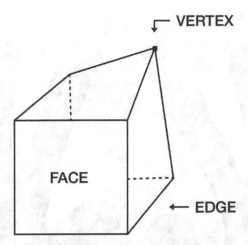

*Figure 1-5.* *A cube diagram showing a transform vertex in 3D space*

3D modeling exists beyond games. As this book is about game development, I continue to cover 3D modeling for games only, since covering all aspects of 3D modeling is beyond the scope of this book.

The job of the 3D modeler is to come up with the best and possibly fastest way to create 3D game assets, by choosing to take a polygonal or sculpting approach. The modeling process usually begins with research and reference gathering. Depending on the art direction or goals, the artist may start with an existing base mesh (3D model), create a mesh from scratch, or use reference images such as concept art. To be an efficient 3D modeler, you should be able to break complex objects into pieces that can be made in 3D space.

Moreover, the job of a 3D modeler is to keep their topology clean, as shown in Figure 1-6. This figure demonstrates the structure, flow, and organization of vertices, edges, and faces. They are ready for the next step in the pipeline, which could be 3D texturing.

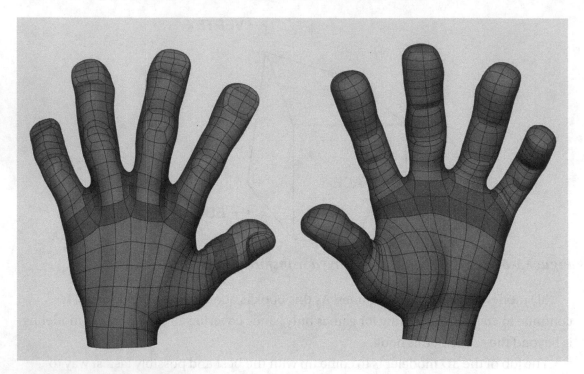

***Figure 1-6.*** *The topology of a stylized hand 3D model by Natalie Asport. Reproduced with permission*

## 3D Texturing

3D texturing is the process of applying 2D images to objects in 3D space. Figure 1-7 shows a 2D layout of a texture that will eventually be applied to a 3D organic model (Figure 1-8). To achieve this, you utilize a texturing program. Regardless of which texturing program you use (such as Substance Painter, 3D Coat, or Quixel), the principles are similar.

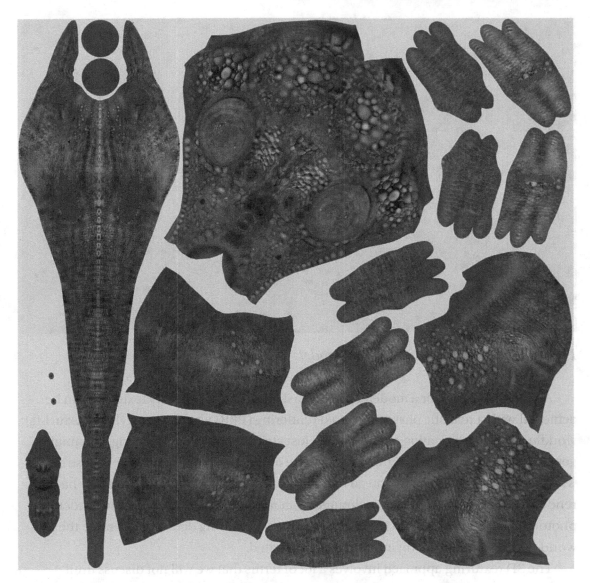

***Figure 1-7.*** *A 2D texture layout of a 3D organic model by Natalie Asport. Reproduced with permission*

***Figure 1-8.*** *A textured 3D organic model*

A 3D texture artist or a modeler may be tasked with texturing. 3D texturing can be achieved with a realistic physically based rendering (PBR) workflow, a stylized texturing workflow, or a combination of both. When just starting out in 3D modeling, you might get intimidated if you do not understand some of the terminology; however, these terms will become more familiar as you go more in-depth in a later chapter. Physically based rendering is a process that uses techniques that mimic real-world lighting to render photorealistic 3D models. On the contrary, stylized texturing does not resemble the real world and its color and form are usually exaggerated.

The 3D texturing approach involves a lot of terms that we will not discuss until Chapter 4; this includes UV mapping, roughness and normal maps, and materials, which are shown in Figure 1-9.

What this chapter discusses is how 3D texturing works in games. I continue to discuss 3D texturing for games only, since covering all aspects of 3D texturing is beyond the scope of this book.

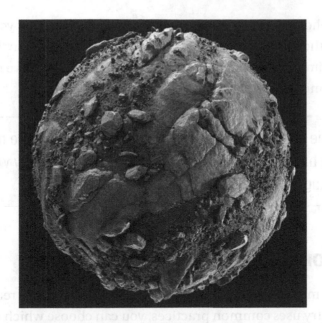

***Figure 1-9.*** *3D texture material by James Ritossa. Reproduced with permission*

The job of the 3D texture artist is to come up with the best tactic in creating efficient texture maps with a believable representation of the material they are depicting. Just like with the 3D modeler, a lot of research is done before starting. Also, depending on the art direction or goals, 3D texture artists may start with smart materials, create materials from scratch, or use scanned photographic material. To be an efficient 3D texture artist, you should be able to break complex real-world materials into pieces that can be represented in 3D space.

The job of a 3D texture artist is to keep their textures optimized and ready for the next step in the pipeline—implementing the textures into a game engine.

## Wait! What About Rigging and Animation?

There is an assumption that rigging and animation happen directly after the modeling stage. However, you could take your 3D model and textures and add them to a game engine if you wanted to, without finishing the entire pipeline. This would be beneficial to see how things look with lights and shadows by rendering everything. It is common practice to do this without textures as part of creating a game's first playable prototype.

The more placeholder art you have to playtest with, the better off you are. Placeholder art, as the name implies, holds the place for something in the future that will be refined and implemented into the final game, such as primitive representations, unpolished art, or finished preexisting art.

---

**Tip**    A lot of game engines can replace 3D models with the same name. This means that if you have placeholder art, you can swap it out easily with updated art. This way of working is very efficient.

---

# Textures Before Rigging or the Other Way?

When you become more knowledgeable with the pipeline, you will realize that although the industry uses common practices, you can choose which stages you want to do before others. Hopefully, by the end of this book, you will have a better grasp of the reasons the industry chooses its pipeline path. An artist could pass on their placeholder model to a technical animator so that they can work on the rig of the model while it is being simultaneously worked on by the artist for the model's textures. Since this is true, we could begin 3D rigging after 3D texturing. For now, we cover rigging. Figure 1-10 shows a rig.

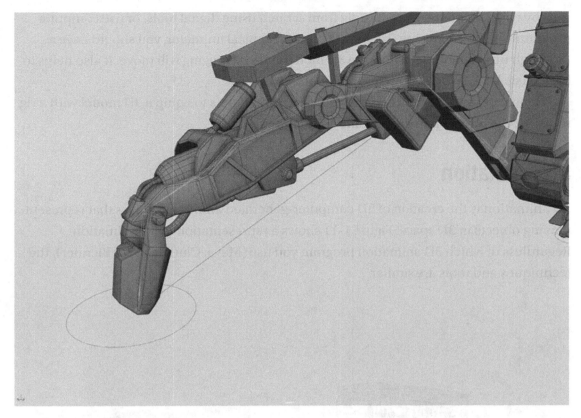

***Figure 1-10.*** *3D rigged robot leg*

3D rigging is the process of creating interconnected skeletal systems using a digital application as a medium to control the movement of objects in 3D space. Similar rigging techniques and tools can be achieved in different software, including Maya, 3ds Max, and Blender.

A technical games animator creates rigs for models made by a 3D artist that will later be used by an animator to animate. The basic process of rigging involves the creation of digital bones, called *joints* in 3D space.

Just like texturing, rigging exists beyond games. Also, a technical animator does more than rigging; however, I will only cover rigging for games, since covering all aspects of technical animators is beyond the scope of this book.

The job of the technical animator is to provide the animator with the best possible setup for them to be able to transform models such as characters and props to the desired positions. Usually, a lot of communication between the modeler, animator, and technical animator will take place. Depending on the art direction or goals, they may start by using an *auto-rig,* create a rig from scratch using digital tools, or use computer programming to create one. To be an efficient technical animator, you should have a thorough understanding of how the 3D models you are rigging will move. It also helps to have basic knowledge of how 3D animation works.

Hence, the main overall task of a technical animator is to equip a 3D model with a rig ready for the next step in the pipeline—3D animation.

## 3D Animation

3D animation is the creation of 3D computer-generated animated images that represent moving objects in 3D space. Figure 1-11 shows a representation of 3D animation. Regardless of which 3D animation program you use (Maya, Cinema4D, or Blender), the techniques and tools are similar.

***Figure 1-11.*** *3D animation stages of a mech model showing two keyframe poses*

A 3D games animator animates 3D models that fall into two main categories: character animation and prop animation. Character animation is the process of bringing characters to life. It includes using movement to tell a story, express emotion, or convey personality. Prop animation also adds movement, but to objects within the game. The fundamental process of 3D animation involves recording keyframes at a given position, rotation, and scale of 3D objects, as shown in Figure 1-12. We discuss creating such keyframes in Chapter 9.

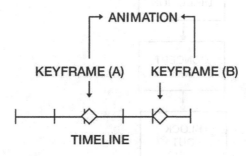

***Figure 1-12.*** *Animation keyframes*

Just as with 3D texturing, 3D animation exists beyond games. As this book is about game development, I only cover 3D animation for games, since covering all aspects of animation is beyond the scope of this book.

The job of the games animator is to re-create believable movement that gives the illusion that the objects are alive. To be a successful character animator, you should be able to convey personality in your character in a 3D space. To achieve this, depending on the creative direction, you need to do research before starting, such as recording someone acting out the movement.

Furthermore, the job of an animator is to keep their keyframes efficient and use only what's needed for possible adjustments, revisions, and game optimization. This approach creates a workflow that is nondestructive and easily iterative within a 3D pipeline.

# The Game Development Workflow

Figure 1-13 shows a flowchart of the 3D game development asset pipeline. The workflow shows the full process, from creative direction to the implementation into a game engine.

As a general principle, you start by doing research, gathering references, and obtaining concept art and art direction. Second, your reference or concept art must be added to the 3D software to create a mesh. Third, you UV map and texture the low poly mesh. Then, you create a rig for the mesh that you can use for animation. Lastly, you export the mesh with textures and animation for integration into a game engine.

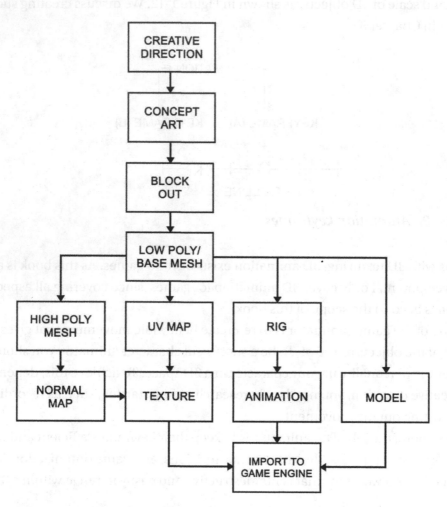

***Figure 1-13.*** *3D asset development pipeline flowchart*

Here is a brief description of each stage illustrated in Figure 1-13:

- **Creative Direction:** The overall vision of the game. This includes game and narrative design, gameplay, and visual and audio direction.

- **Concept Art:** 2D or 3D art that conveys an idea or creative direction. This stage is usually done in pre-production.

- **Block-Out:** Usually grayscale, textureless primitive geometry used to block out the level design of a game and used as a general asset placeholder. Block-outs are mainly used in early prototypes.

- **Mesh:** A game model asset can go through phases such as a base mesh and high poly.

  - **Base Mesh:** An object that has been modeled, often with few features and no texture mapping. For this reason, it is a starting point for 3D models.

  - **Low Poly Mesh:** A polygon mesh that intentionally is made up of a relatively small amount of polygons (polys) and usually has a set poly limit to keep it from going over. It captures the reads that affect silhouette and detail that must be modeled. This mesh is often used as the in-game mesh since its low density makes it ideal for real-time rendering.

  - **High Poly Mesh:** In contrast to the low poly mesh, a high poly mesh contains a large amount of polygons, which allows for more detail. The higher the poly count, the longer it takes to render; therefore in the context of real-time graphics, this mesh will be used mainly for texture baking and creation for the low poly mesh.

---

**Tip**    From the following meshes, sometimes one mesh can take the place of another in different contexts.

---

- **Texture:** These are images referred to as texture maps applied to the 3D model that represent a given material. Some texture maps include:

  - **Base Color Map:** A texture that displays diffuse or flat color information.

  - **Normal Map:** A technique that uses fake lighting to create details such as wrinkles, dents, and bumps.

- **UV Layout:** How a 2D image is wrapped around a 3D model. The process of projecting the image to the 3D model.

- **Rig:** Interconnected joints with controls used to animate a 3D model.

- **Animation:** The illusion of an inanimate object being alive, created by combining a series of images or frames.

- **Integrate into Game Engine:** This last stage depicts bringing a 3D model, its textures, and animation into the game engine.

# Working with a Team

You may first start out working solo on 3D art for games as you learn the craft. Then, you may expand to working as part of a team. If you end up working with a team, it is important to communicate. This should happen as much as possible. Figure 1-14 shows the typical workflow with a technical animator, 3D modeler, and 3D animator.

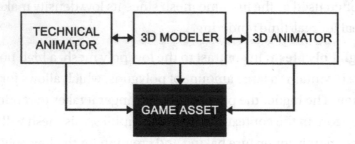

***Figure 1-14.*** *Communication workflow among 3D artists*

Everyone on the team needs to work together to create game assets. For instance, animators might need a rig to provide movements not common for a particular 3D asset, but they would not know about this unless it was expressed to them.

The 3D modeler might realize that something that the animator wants is not possible without customization. For example, a character arm model that requires squash and stretch functionality needs geometry that supports that feature. Or perhaps the animator wants the 3D modeler to position the default pose of a 3D character in a certain way. Without constant communication, unwanted issues might present themselves later.

Figure 1-15 shows the same workflow from 3D artists, including a larger team from the game director to the playtesters. This illustrates how game development is not a linear pipeline and how you are part of this working process. Even when there is communication with other artists, this does not mean that the assets are final. They will require further approval, such as from a game director after a playtest. Then, you might receive revisions or feedback from art leads who communicate with the game director.

For now, as you work independently through the chapters in this book, realize that understanding all these roles will benefit you during every step in the pipeline. Since there is overlap at every stage, having a decent understanding of specific pipelines or disciplines within the development pipeline will create a stronger final product. This also creates a stronger foundation for communication.

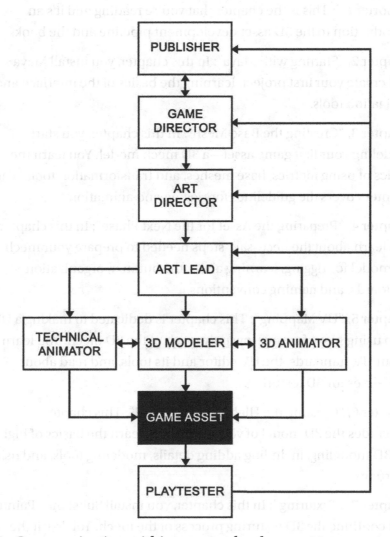

*Figure 1-15.* *Communication within a game development team*

# How to Use This Book

If you're a beginner in both game development and 3D art, it's best to read the book from cover to cover. If you are an advanced 3D artist or want to learn about a specific part of the pipeline, you can jump to any particular chapter that interests you.

The chapters take you through the pipeline of creating a 3D mech with textures and animation to use in a game engine. Here's a brief description of each chapter's topics:

- Chapter 1, "What Is the 3D Production Pipeline and Why Is It Important?": This is the chapter that you're reading and it's an introduction to the 3D asset development pipeline and the book.

- Chapter 2, "Starting with Maya": In this chapter, you install Maya and create your first project, learning the basics of the interface and navigation tools.

- Chapter 3, "Creating the Base Mesh": In this chapter, you start modeling your first game asset—a 3D mech model. You learn the basics of using metrics, base meshes, and transformation tools. The chapter covers the guidelines for rigging and animation.

- Chapter 4, "Preparing the Asset for the Next Phase": In this chapter, you learn about the necessary steps needed to prepare your mech 3D model for rigging, learning about the outliner, organization standards, and naming conventions.

- Chapter 5, "UV Mapping": This chapter is dedicated to making a UV map using Maya for your low poly mesh of the 3D mech. You learn about UV standards, the UV editor and its tools, and read about guidelines for 3D texturing.

- Chapter 6, "Creating the High Poly 3D Model": This chapter concludes the 3D model of your mech. You learn the basics of high-res 3D modeling, including adding details, modeling tools, and using shortcuts.

- Chapter 7, "Texturing": In this chapter, you install Substance Painter and continue the 3D texturing process of the mech. You learn the basics of using layers, baking normal maps, adding details, and using smart materials.

- Chapter 8, "Rigging the Mech" In this chapter, you create your first character rig for your mech asset. You learn about joints, IKs, controllers, control curves, constraints, skin binding, and about cleaning up the rig for animation ease.

- Chapter 9, "Bringing the Asset to Life": This chapter concludes the 3D game mech asset project and is the end of our pipeline. You create an idle animation, install Unity, implement the mech in it, and play the game.

# Nonlinear Game Development

When developing a game, certain tasks have to be done before others. By the same token, games go through an iterative design process, whereby a prototype of a game could be altered. That means that no production process is strictly linear. Therefore, this book points out what things need to be achieved in a certain order and when order doesn't matter.

# Embracing and Utilizing Computer Shortcuts

As a professor in a game design department and as a former computer science teacher, I have encountered many students who were hesitant to use computer shortcuts when they were just starting to learn a new program. This is something that I feel strongly about.

I can see from their point of view that they want to avoid relearning new ways of doing the same things. However, I strongly advise you to get out of your comfort zone and gradually expand your knowledge and skillset with shortcuts.

These shortcuts were created for a reason—to work faster, more efficiently, and to ultimately speed up your workflow. Utilizing new computer shortcuts may not be easy at first, but that work will pay off in the long run. Don't be afraid to be uncomfortable while learning a faster way of doing something.

I would love to introduce shortcuts from the start so that you have no chance of being reluctant. However, because this book is for beginners, I do indicate where shortcuts originate and note their menu locations.

Therefore, I trust that when the time comes and I introduce shortcuts, you will use them. I recall my undergrad professor, Lorna Hernandez, who only showed us shortcuts without showing us where they originated.

> *You can tell that someone is an amateur at using computer software by the lack of their shortcut usage.*
>
> —Lorna Hernandez, Professor

Professor Hernandez was not teaching an introductory course, but I still loved her teaching approach. Using shortcuts is as important as the tools you use.

# Using the Right Tools

What are the *right* tools for the job? This is a question that has been asked many times. The answer is a tricky one because it heavily depends on you and what you want to achieve. You might want to be an independent or AAA 3D artist, hobbyist, or educator. To help you out, Table 1-1 is a comparison of several 3D creation software programs, with the pros and cons. Likewise, Table 1-2 is a game engine software comparison. For fairness, I only list and discuss the most widely used programs. So keep in mind that there are more available options than I cover here.

***Table 1-1.*** *3D Creation Software Comparison*

| Software | Pros | Cons |
|---|---|---|
| 3ds Max | Popular for its powerful modeling tools. It provides an efficient and fast workflow when 3D modeling. | Only available on one platform: Microsoft Windows. |
| Blender | Free to use. It also has an extensive amount of tools that include modeling, animation, sculpting, rigging, texturing, and effects. | Although Blender has a lot of the same features that industry-standard programs have, some tools are missing. |
| Cinema 4D | Popular for motion graphics and has a smooth workflow with programs like After Effects. | It has limited tools for game development. |

*(continued)*

***Table 1-1.*** (*continued*)

| Software | Pros | Cons |
| --- | --- | --- |
| Houdini | Popular for the creation of dynamic and procedural environments, as well as particle effects. | It has a high learning curve and the tools take time to get used to. |
| Marmoset Toolbag | Popular for its rendering tools. It eliminates the need to export assets to an engine and sets the bar for producing quality lit scenes and post-processing effects. | The way that your model looks in Marmoset is not necessarily how it will look in a game engine. |
| Maya | Its scripting languages make this software highly customizable. It also has an extensive amount of 3D tools. It is mainly popular for creating 3D animation. It is also the industry standard for 3D game art. | It has a high learning curve and is very robust, with lots of tools. |
| MayaLT | If you are familiar with using Maya, MayaLT is a condensed version with most of your game development needs. | It does not include all of Maya features, including the rendering and effects tools. |
| Mudbox | Popular for its intuitive 3D sculpting and painting tools. | The number of shapes to sculpt is limited and the program uses a lot of computing power, which limits your 3D sculpting needs. |
| Substance Designer | Popular for its PBR procedural material-creation tools that can be modified at runtime in an indestructible manner. It also integrates well with Substance Painter. | Mainly used for creating materials. |
| Substance Painter | Popular for its PBR painting and smart texturing tools that speed up 3D texturing workflows. It exports textures for most 3D programs. | Mainly used for creating textures. |
| Zbrush | Popular for what seems to be its limitless 3D sculpting tool. | The interface is different than most 3D programs, making it sometimes hard to adapt to. |

**Table 1-2.** *Game Engine Software Comparison*

| Software | Pros | Cons |
|---|---|---|
| Game Maker | Does not require programming knowledge to make a game. | Has a limited scripting language. |
| Godot | Free to use. | Does not have the number of features and rendering quality that other popular game engines offer. |
| Unity | Popular for its 2D and 3D multi-platform tools. It has been used by many popular indie games. | Has frequent drastic updates that could break your build if you upgrade. |
| Unreal Engine | Popular for its realistic rendering. It has also been used to develop popular AAA games. | Due to its high performance, it requires powerful hardware and a graphics card to work optimally. |

This book covers the 3D asset game development pipeline using Maya, Substance Painter, and the Unity Game Engine.

Although I chose these specific applications, I do my best to explain the 3D asset pipeline regardless of the tools you use.

# What Is Maya?

Maya is the 3D software shown in Figure 1-16. It includes modeling, animation, rendering, simulation, and texturing tools. At the time of writing this book, it is the industry-leading 3D animation software program. I was developed by Autodesk and is used for animating films, visual effects, and digital games.

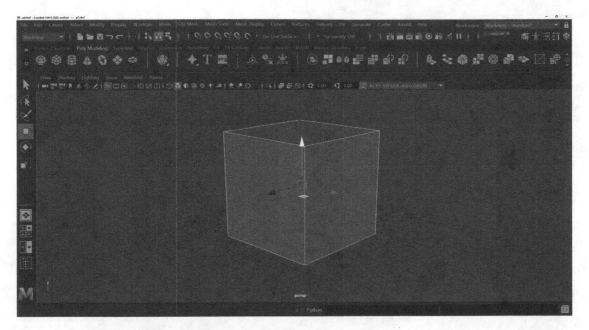

*Figure 1-16.* *Screenshot of Autodesk Maya*

## What Is Substance Painter?

Substance Painter is the 3D texturing software shown in Figure 1-17. It includes painting, smart materials, baking, rendering, and texturing tools. It uses smart masks and procedural texturing tools, which help speed up your workflow. At the time of writing of this book, it is the industry-leading 3D painting software application. It was developed by Allegorithmic and is used for animated films, visual effects, and digital games.

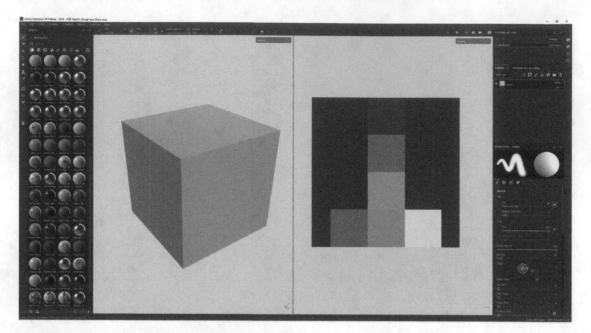

*Figure 1-17. Screenshot of Substance Painter*

## What Is Unity?

Unity is the 2D and 3D cross-platform game engine shown in Figure 1-18. It includes graphics, physics, audio, and a rendering engine. It has become popular due to its ease of use and its support for more than 25 platforms. That includes Windows, Mac, iOS, Android, PlayStation, and Xbox. At the time of writing this book, it is the leading independent developer game engine application. It was developed by Unity Technology and is used for digital games, virtual reality, augmented reality, simulations, and animated films.

*Figure 1-18.* *Screenshot of Unity*

# Pricing

What is great about Maya, Substance Painter, and Unity is that they all have free-to-use educational licenses. Table 1-3 compares the different licenses.

*Table 1-3.* *Game Development Software*

| Software | License | Developer | Popular Features |
|---|---|---|---|
| 3ds Max | Educational, Commercial | Autodesk | Modeling, animation, simulation, lighting, rendering |
| Blender | GNU (Free, General Public) | Blender Foundation | Modeling, animation, texturing, rigging, sculpting, simulation, lighting, rendering, 2D/3D toon animation |
| Cinema 4D | Educational, Commercial | MAXON | Animation, lighting, modeling visual 3D effects, rendering, simulation |

(*continued*)

***Table 1-3.*** (*continued*)

| Software | License | Developer | Popular Features |
|---|---|---|---|
| Houdini | Educational, Indie, Commercial | Side Effects Software | Animation, lighting, modeling, visual 3D effects |
| Marmoset Toolbag | Commercial | Marmoset | Rendering, animation, baking |
| Maya | Educational, Indie, Commercial | Autodesk | Modeling, animation, lighting, rigging rendering, visual 3D effects |
| MayaLT | Educational, Commercial | Autodesk | Modeling, animation, rigging |
| Mudbox | Educational, Commercial | Autodesk | Sculpting, lighting |
| Substance Designer | Educational, Indie, Pro, Enterprise | Allegorithmic, owned by Adobe | Material creation |
| Substance Painter | Educational, Indie, Pro, Enterprise | Allegorithmic, owned by Adobe | Texturing |
| Unity | Personal, Indie, Pro, Enterprise | Unity Technologies | Cross-platform, 2D and 3D graphics, virtual reality, physics, simulation, rendering |
| Unreal Engine | Free until the game succeeds | Epic | cross-platform, 2D and 3D graphics, virtual reality, physics, simulation, rendering |
| Zbrush | Educational, Commercial | Pixologic | Sculpting, modeling, texturing, lighting, rendering |

# Getting Started

Having come this far, you should be ready to start thinking about the first part of the project you will be working on in this book. This first part is the pre-production phase, where you do research and gather references.

# The Importance of Using References

Do not hesitate to use references. Especially if you are starting your career as a 3D artist, you can greatly improve your artistic capabilities simply by looking at sources of inspiration.

On the other hand, an amateur 3D artist is easily spotted when they do not utilize reference images, regardless of whether they started recently or years ago. Let's consider why you need to use references and how you gather them.

Let's say needed to 3D model a vintage typewriter. Using your memory alone, take one minute to note all of the details that you can think of that are found on a vintage typewriter.

Keep thinking.

How did you do? Did you miss the typewheel, feed roller, platen knob, and ribbon reverse button (see Figure 1-20)? Do you know what these are? Unless you have a strong familiarity with typewriters (or a photographic memory), most likely you will not be able to accurately remember their details.

Like most of the information we pick up from the world around us, we retain a portion of what we take in. We usually cannot recollect all the nuanced details, especially later. Therefore, if you use a reference, it provides a clearer picture of what needs to be modeled and can eliminate the guesswork. Besides, 3D artists tend to work faster with references and avoid pitfalls like making inaccurate models.

For instance, say a player comes across a vehicle that has the wrong scale, or the mirrors are in the wrong place, or the door hinges are at a weird angle, or the wheels are in an impossible position. Players can sense something is off even if they may not be a vehicle expert. The main thing is to make sure your choices are intentional and not simply due to lack of knowledge of the subject matter. Knowing your subject matter can be as simple as gathering references.

# Gathering References

To gather references, you need to do your research. The goal is for the reference material to clearly show how an asset, environment, action, or expression should look from as many angles as possible. It is standard practice to use orthographic images if available, which show the front, side, bottom, and/or top views. Figure 1-19 shows some orthographic views.

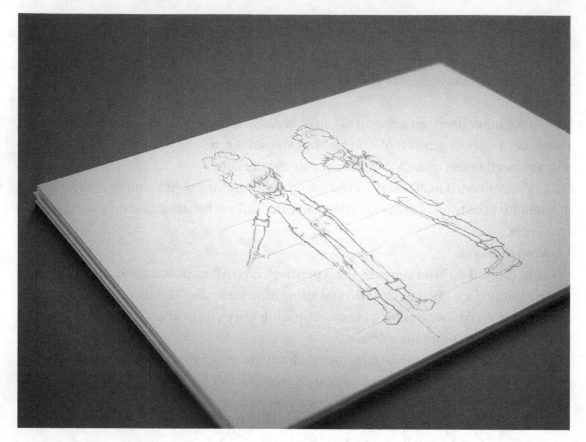

***Figure 1-19.*** *Concept art of a character design drawn in orthographic views*

Ideally, you could be 3D modeling an asset or an environment for a game. If so, take a lot of photographic or video references of the asset, as shown in Figure 1-20. This is how the vintage typewriter that I previously mentioned looks.

***Figure 1-20.*** *Photograph of a vintage typewriter*

If, for instance, you are working on character animation, recording footage of you or someone else acting the actions out is a great way to obtain a reference. This technique is not new to the industry, but a common one that has been around for years. Nowadays, you can even find online animation references for your game, such as idle, walking, running, and jumping cycles.

However, you may not always have access to reference art or can't find existing photographs or videos that will work. Figure 1-21 shows concept art that an artist could provide at the start of creating an asset.

***Figure 1-21.*** *Concept art of robots*

In the pipeline, once you have your concept art to follow and have gathered your references, you can move onto starting your model. With your concept art and an overview of the pipeline, you are ready to start using the first program needed for the next step in the pipeline. This is covered in the following chapter.

# Summary

This chapter covered an overview and an introduction to the 3D asset game development pipeline. It looked at the different roles and tasks of 3D artists. You started to learn what 3D modeling, texturing, rigging, and animation are and how they all fit in the 3D pipeline. The chapter then covered the tools necessary to complete these stages. Then, you read about the importance of gathering references. Finally, the chapter briefly described each step in the pipeline and explained how they correspond to game development as a whole.

# CHAPTER 2

# Starting with Maya

In this chapter, you install Maya and create your first primitive shapes with it, learning the basics of the interface and the navigation tools. You might be tempted to rush through this chapter so you can get to your first project. However, this chapter explains important techniques that you'll need in Chapter 3. I suggest you go over each section as many times as you need before starting the next chapter.

## Installing and Opening Maya

Download Maya from `www.autodesk.com` and install it. Free trial, educational, and professional versions are available. All the different licenses offer full features. You need to create a new account with Autodesk before you can download the product. When you run the program the first time, you'll need to register the product's license following the prompts. I used Maya 2020 at the time of writing this book.

If you add Maya's shortcut app to your desktop, you can double-click the program's icon to start it. Maya can also be open from the Windows Start menu by choosing ➤ Programs ➤ Maya, and on the Mac, by choosing Applications ➤ Maya.

After Maya starts, the What's New Highlight Settings window (shown in Figure 2-1) will open. You can close it by clicking OK.

© Nova Villanueva 2022
N. Villanueva, *Beginning 3D Game Assets Development Pipeline*,
https://doi.org/10.1007/978-1-4842-7196-4_2

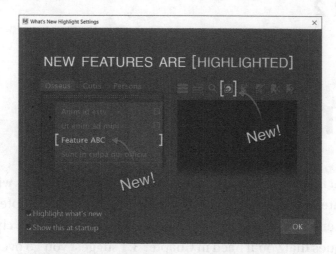

**Figure 2-1.** *Maya's What's New Highlights Settings window*

# Overview of the Interface

Maya consists of several windows that can be repositioned. The interface includes a top menu, menu sets, shelves, a channel box, a view panel (or scene view), and a Time Slider. I briefly discuss the interface in this chapter and then explain more as needed throughout the book.

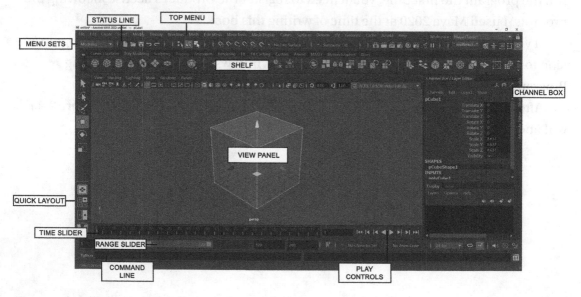

**Figure 2-2.** *Screenshot of Maya's interface*

# Menu Sets

Menu sets come in Modeling, Rigging, Animation, FX, and Rendering categories. The menus change depending on the menu set you choose. In this chapter, you will use the default modeling menu shown in Figure 2-3.

*Figure 2-3.  Modeling menu set*

# The Top Menu

The top menu, shown in Figure 2-4, is the main menu that sits at the top of the Maya program window. I refer to this menu a lot throughout this book.

*Figure 2-4.  Top menu*

# Shelves

Think of shelves (see Figure 2-5) as visual shortcut menus in Maya. They include icons for common tasks, organized by tabs based on category. What is great about shelves is that you can customize them by adding your own items.

*Figure 2-5.  Poly Modeling shelf*

# The Channel Box

The Channel Box (see Figure 2-6) allows you to edit attributes such as changing an object's scale size and its key value for animation purposes. It is important to know that there are more attributes than are shown by default and you can create your own.

*Figure 2-6.*  *The Channel Box*

# Quick Layout/Outliner Buttons

The top three Quick Layout buttons (see Figure 2-7) allow you to switch between the View panel (Figure 2-11) layouts with a single click. The bottom button opens the Outliner.

*Figure 2-7.*  *Top three Quick Layout buttons*

# The Time Slider

The Time Slider (see Figure 2-8) shows you the time range that is available as defined by the length of the range slider (see Figure 2-9). This panel is mainly use for animation purposes. The Time Slider also displays the current time and the keys on selected objects or characters. Chapter 9 covers the Time Slider more.

***Figure 2-8.*** *The Time Slider*

# The Range Slider

The Range Slider (see Figure 2-9) lets you set the start and end times of the scene's animation. You can also set a playback range if you want to focus on a smaller portion of the whole animation.

***Figure 2-9.*** *The Range Slider*

# Playback Controls

The Playback Controls (see Figure 2-10) let you move around time and preview your animation as defined by the Time Slider range.

***Figure 2-10.*** *Playback controls*

# The View Panel

The View Panel (see Figure 2-11) shows you a preview of your scene from the perspective or orthographic view. Using this panel, you can create, form, and edit 3D meshes.

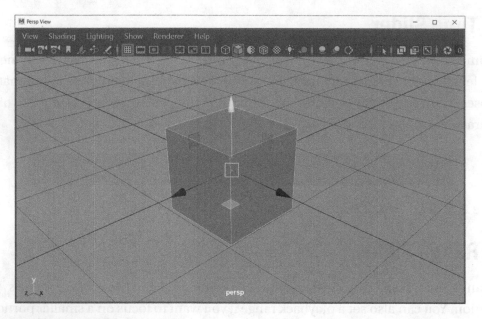

***Figure 2-11.*** *The View Panel*

# Creating Primitives

Maya comes with several primitive shapes, including Sphere, Cube, Cylinder, Cone, and Torus. A modeler will typically start out with a primitive shape and adapt its form using the tools we cover in Chapter 4. For the most part, the game industry uses polygons; therefore, throughout this book, I focus on them. Let's practice making primitives.

In the top menu, choose Create ➤ Polygon Primitive, and choose the primitive type or select the primitive from the Polygon shelf. Then choose Create ➤ Polygon Primitives ➤ Cube. See Figure 2-12.

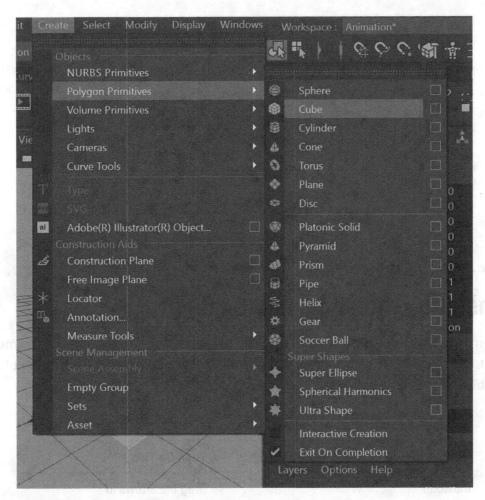

***Figure 2-12.*** *Choosing the Cube shape*

The primitive is created in the center of the grid, as shown in Figure 2-13. The edges are light green if the object is selected in Object Mode. When you are in Object Mode, you can translate, scale, or rotate the entire object. Later chapters cover other modes for editing primitives and meshes.

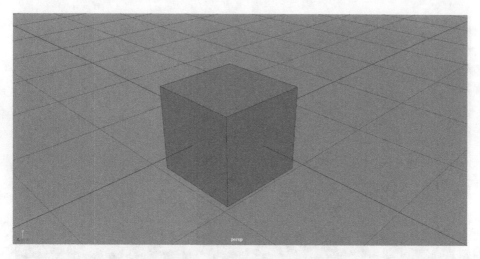

***Figure 2-13.*** *The cube primitive*

# Translating, Rotating, and Scaling

You can move, scale, or rotate a mesh by using the shortcuts. For this to work, the mesh needs to be selected. Then you press W to translate, E to rotate, and R to scale the object. See Table 2-1.

***Table 2-1.*** *Navigation Controls*

| Transform | Press Before Using | Then Do This |
|---|---|---|
| Translate | W | Drag the arrows in your desired axis (x, y, or z) |
| Rotate | E | Drag the circles in |
| Scale | R | your desired axis (x, y, or z) Drag the cubes in your desired axis (x, y, or z) |

You should practice creating more primitives and transforming them. It is important to practice moving objects in Maya using the arrows. This keeps your object on a given axis and you won't randomly end up somewhere in the world. This will make more sense when you read about navigation in the next section, where instead of moving the objects, you move around the scene. Figures 2-14, 2-15, and 2-16 show the results of translating, rotating, and scaling the cube, respectively.

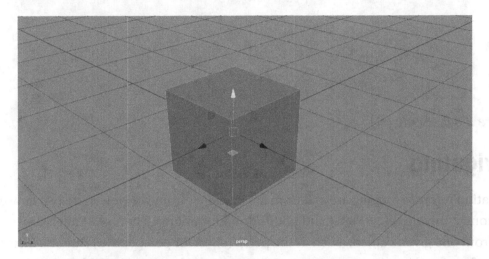

***Figure 2-14.*** *Translate (W)*

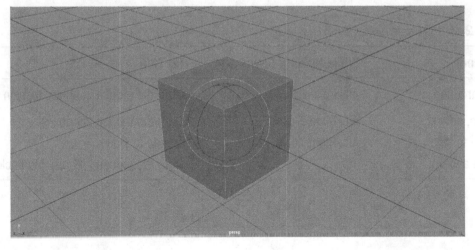

***Figure 2-15.*** *Rotate (E)*

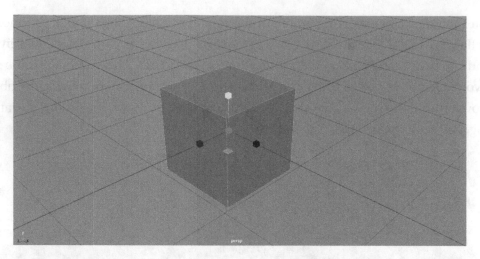

*Figure 2-16.* *Scale (R)*

# Navigating

Navigation refers to looking around from any camera through a view panel. So far we mentioned only the View Panel and nothing about cameras. The View Panels are only seen from one given camera, such as the persp (short for perspective) camera. Instead of transforming the cube, you can use navigation to look around it. Table 2-2 covers the controls needed to rotate, track, and zoom around the cube.

*Table 2-2.* *Navigation Controls*

| Movement | While Holding Down... | Do This |
| --- | --- | --- |
| Rotate around | Alt+Left-click | Drag the mouse in an arc fashion |
| Track up, down, and side to side | Alt+Middle-click Alt+Right-click | Drag the mouse up, down, or side to side |
| Zoom in and out | | Drag the mouse forward and back |

# Duplicating Objects

Instead of creating new primitives, you can duplicate any object in the scene. With the object selected, do the following:

1.  Press Ctrl+D.

2.  The duplicate will appear in the same place as the original. You can press W to translate it.

3.  You can also choose Edit ➤ Duplicate in the top menu.

4.  While in transform (W) mode, you can also hold Shift and drag a clone. See Figure 2-17.

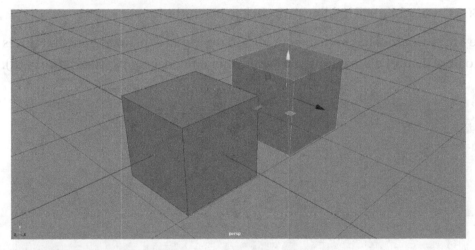

***Figure 2-17.*** *Duplicated cube*

# Deleting Objects

I am sure by now you have a bunch of primitives you created and are wondering how to delete them. To delete one, with the object selected, choose Edit ➤ Delete in the top menu or press the Delete key.

# Adding Edge Loops

Edge loops help define the form of an object. Primitives are your starting shape. Adding edge loops to them allows you to adapt their structure. There are multiple ways to add edges to objects, but the most powerful way is to use the Multi-Cut tool.

If you deleted all your primitives from the previous exercises, create a new one so you can add an edge loop to it. To insert an edge loop with the Multi-Cut tool, follow these steps:

1.  In the top menu, choose Mesh Tools ➤ Multi-Cut tool.

2.  If your object was not selected, you can click it to enable the Multi-Cut tool on it. Then, hold Ctrl and drag your cursor across the mesh to preview your edge loop.

3.  Then, while still holding Ctrl, click to insert the loop.

The Multi-Cut tool has more functions and uses than explained here, but this is a far as we go here. Later I discuss how you can further edit edge loops (see Figure 2-18).

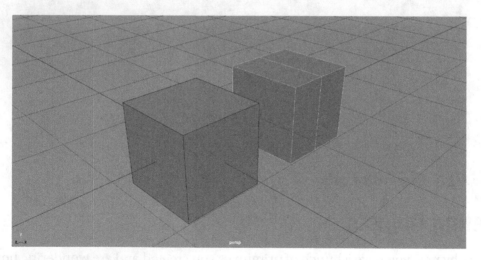

*Figure 2-18.*  *Edge loop on a cube*

# Pivoting

As you may have noticed, when you translated, rotated, or scale a primitive, movement occurred from its center. This is because primitives have a center pivot. A *pivot* is defined as the position were the object is transformed from. It comes in handy when you want to move the object's pivot location. You can change a pivot by doing the following:

1. Select the primitive object.

2. Choose a transform tool (W, E, or R).

3. Press D.

4. When a new transform manipulator appears, move the arrows on any given axis to the desired location. What you are moving is the pivot (see Figure 2-19).

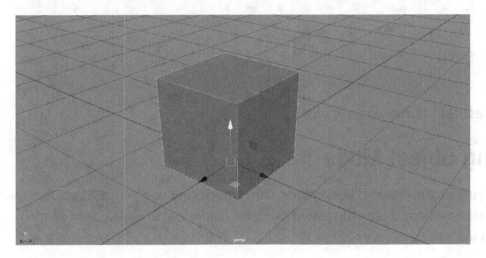

***Figure 2-19.*** *A cube's pivot*

# Mirroring

When modeling complex objects, it is common practice to use a mirroring technique. When an object is symmetrical, a modeler only has to work on one side, then duplicate it to use as the other side, as shown in Figure 2-20. This saves a lot of time. Even if the object will be asymmetrical, the modeler can still use this technique, then modify one side thereafter.

It is important to note that the mirroring will take place from the object's pivot location. It is common to work in the center of the grid and snap the pivot (by holding and pressing X) to its center. Figure 2-19 shows the pivot in the center of the grid where the face was mirrored over.

There are multiple ways to mirror geometry. The simplest way is to duplicate it (Ctrl+D), as you previously learned, and use the Channel Box window to edit the Scale X to -1. This mirrors the geometry over the X axis. The Y or Z axis can also be chosen.

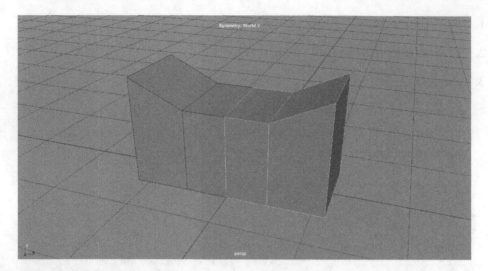

*Figure 2-20.* *Mirrored geometry*

# Using Object Mode

So far you have only seen Object Mode. Other modes include Vertex, Edge, Face, and UV. You can switch modes by right-clicking the object and drag-selecting another, as shown in Figure 2-21.

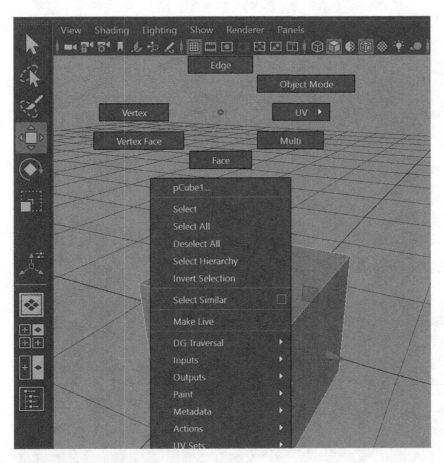

*Figure 2-21.*  *Selection Mode menu*

# Editing Faces, Vertexes, and Edges

To be able to further adapt the forms of your primitive objects, you can edit their faces, vertices, and edges. If you switch to any of these modes, you can utilize the transform tools (W, E, R) to manipulate them. Figures 2-22, 2-23, and 2-24 show Face mode, Vertex mode, and Edge mode, respectively.

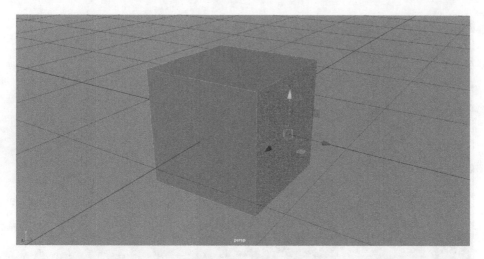

***Figure 2-22.*** *Face mode*

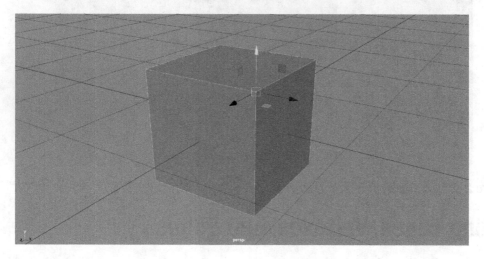

***Figure 2-23.*** *Vertex mode*

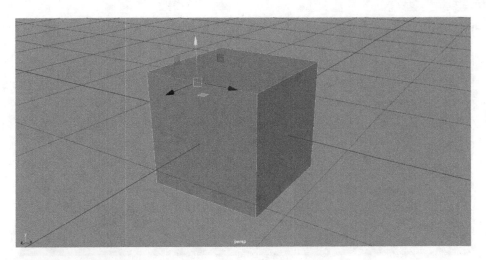

**Figure 2-24.** *Edge mode*

# Selecting Objects

There are different ways you can select faces, vertices, and edges. Here are the basics:

- Drag-select multiple faces, vertices, or edges at once.

- Click them to select them individually.

- Hold down Shift and select more than one at a time. Figure 2-25 shows multiple selected faces and Figure 2-26 shows multiple selected vertices.

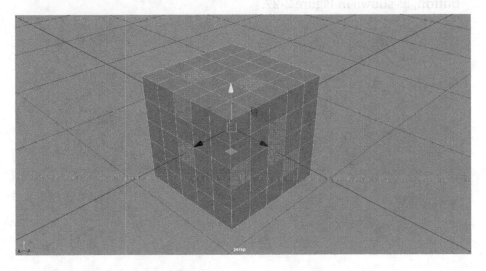

**Figure 2-25.** *Multiple selected faces*

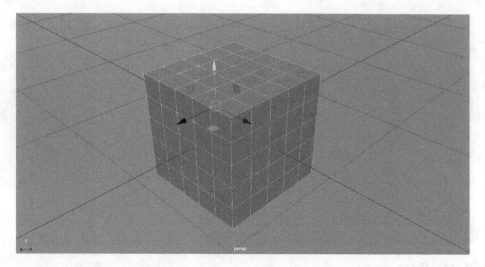

***Figure 2-26.*** *Multiple selected vertices*

# Deleting Faces, Vertices, and Edges

Similar to deleting objects as a whole, you can delete any face or vertex by doing the following:

1. In the top menu, choose Edit ➤ Delete or press the Delete key.

2. For Edges, this method is not sufficient. If you simply delete them this way, you will run into issues in the geometry. Instead, you hold Shift and right-click then drag on top of the Delete Edge button, as shown in Figure 2-27.

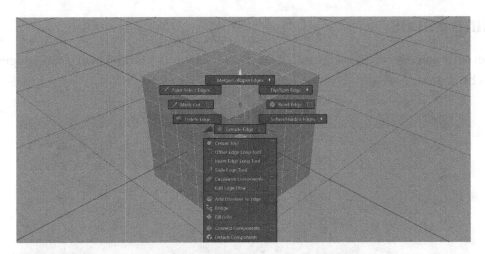

**Figure 2-27.** *Marquee menu with Delete Edge*

# Transforming Faces, Vertices, and Edges

You can transform (W) vertices, faces, and edges, as shown in Figure 2-28.

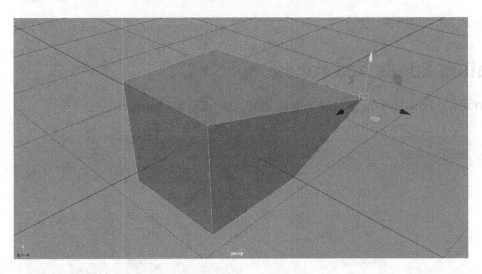

**Figure 2-28.** *Vertex transformation*

# Scaling Faces

You can only scale faces (see Figure 2-29) outside of Object Mode. Vertices and edges cannot be scaled.

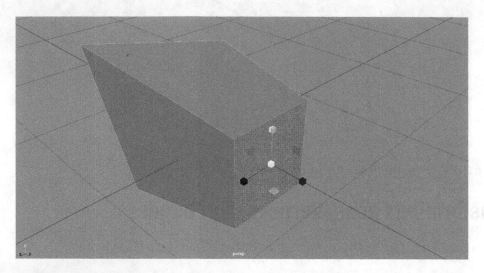

***Figure 2-29.***   *Face scaling*

# Rotating Edges and Faces

And finally, edges and faces (see Figure 2-30) can only be rotated.

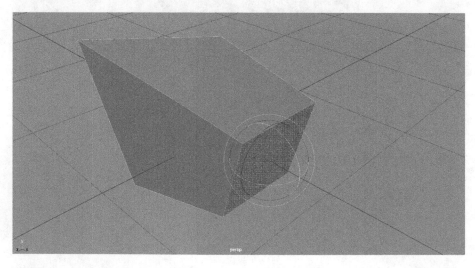

***Figure 2-30.***   *Face rotation*

## Duplicating Faces

Create a new cube (choose Create ➤ Polygonal Primitives ➤ Cube) to see how to duplicate a face. Then follow these steps:

1. Right-click and drag to select Face Mode.

2. Select the top face of the cube.

3. With the face selected, choose Edit Mesh ➤ Duplicate in the top menu.

4. Use the transform arrows to move your face up, as shown in Figure 2-31.

5. To get out of the Duplicate tool, click anywhere in the scene without selecting any other objects.

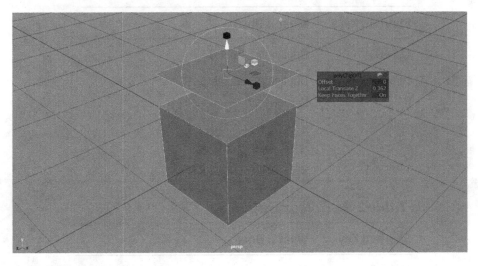

***Figure 2-31.*** *Duplicated face*

## Before Continuing

Make sure you understand and can do all the basic techniques covered so far before you keep going. Specifically, be sure you can move around the scene by using the Alt key and a mouse. This navigation is not an easy thing to master. It takes time and practice. Everything covered in this chapter is used to build a Mech model in the following chapter.

# Maya Shortcuts

The following tables are not a complete list of Maya's shortcuts but show the commonly used shortcut keys by category. Throughout this book I explain what they are used for.

***Table 2-3.*** *Tool/Outliner Operations*

| Shortcut Keys | What It Does |
| --- | --- |
| W | Move tool |
| E | Rotate tool |
| R | Scale tool |
| G | Performs the last command |
| F | Centers the selected object |

***Table 2-4.*** *Edit Operations*

| Shortcut Keys | What It Does |
| --- | --- |
| Ctrl+D | Duplicate |
| Ctrl+Shift+D | Duplicate Special |
| P | Parent |
| Shift+P | Unparent |
| Ctrl+S | Save Scene |
| Ctrl+Shift+S | Save Scene As |

***Table 2-5.*** *Hotbox Display*

| Shortcut Keys | What It Does |
| --- | --- |
| (Hold) Space | Shows the Hotbox menu |

***Table 2-6.*** *Snapping Operation*

| Shortcut Keys | What It Does |
| --- | --- |
| (Hold) J | Move, Rotate, and Scale tool snapping |
| (Hold) C | Snap to curves |
| (Hold) X | Snap to the grid |
| (Hold) V | Snap to points (vertices/joints) |

**Table 2-7.**  *Display Settings*

| Shortcut Keys | What It Does |
|---|---|
| 4 | Wireframe |
| 5 | Shaded display |

**Table 2-8.**  *Animation Shortcuts*

| Shortcut Keys | What It Does |
|---|---|
| S | Set Key |
| Shift+E | Set Key at Rotate |
| Shift+R | Set Key at Scale |
| Shift+W | Set Key at Translate |

# Setting Up the Project

You can now start to set up the Mech project. Since Maya depends on multiple resources from different locations, your projects will let the program keep track of all the files needed for your scene by storing them in one location.

## Setting Up the Mech Project

1.  Create a folder somewhere on your computer that you have easy access to it and name it Mech.

2.  Open the Mech folder and create two new folders inside of it, named Textures and Scenes. Make sure you spell Scenes correctly because Maya will need to identify it.

3.  Back in Maya, do not worry if you have objects from the previous steps or if you have a blank scene. This will not matter. In the top menu, choose File ➤ Set Project.

4.  Navigate to the Mech folder you created in Step 1.

5.  Click Set.

6. Create a new blank scene (choose File ➤ New Scene or press Ctrl+N)

7. A warning dialog box will appear, asking you to Save Changes to Untitled Scene. You can choose Don't Save unless you want your first creations.

8. A blank new scene should open.

9. Then save it as Mech1 (choose File ➤ Save or press Ctrl+S). If you set the project up correctly, the Scenes folder should open. This is where you save Mech1. If it does not work, do not panic. Try to set it up again from Step 3.

# Summary

This chapter covered an overview and a brief introduction to Maya's interface and navigation. You started to learn about basic modeling techniques. You looked at the different ways objects can be manipulated, including transform, rotation, and scale. You also learned about Object, Face, Vertex and Edge mode, to understand how a mesh's form can be further adapted. Finally, you set up a project that you will use throughout this book.

# CHAPTER 3

# Creating a Base Mesh

In this chapter, you start to make a game asset and a 3D mech. You learn the basics of using metrics, base meshes, and transformation tools. You also read about the guidelines for rigging and animation. You will continue with this project throughout the entire book to cover the asset's pipeline. As shown in Figure 3-1, the Base or Low Poly mesh is the first component of making a game asset.

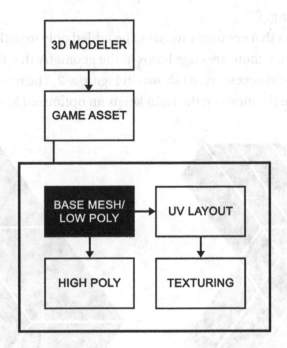

*Figure 3-1.* *A 3D modeler process flowchart*

© Nova Villanueva 2022
N. Villanueva, *Beginning 3D Game Assets Development Pipeline*,
https://doi.org/10.1007/978-1-4842-7196-4_3

# Creating a Base Mesh

A 3D modeler will either start with an existing low polygon mesh or will create their own. When you start learning 3D, it is recommended to create your own as you will learn about proper topology and acquire basic modeling skills. After you learn the basics, it is common practice to use existing base meshes, such as a low poly mesh of a character, and then adapt it to the character you are making. In the beginning, you may be tempted to use an existing base mesh, but then you may not have the essential skills to properly adapt the shape.

For this base mesh, it is important to keep the poly count to a minimum. This allows the modeler to quickly make changes to the overall shape and facilitates the animation and texturing processes. However, when you are just learning about modeling, it is hard to determine what a low poly count is because it heavily depends on what you are making.

My rule of thumb is that geometry needs to be added only to define the form and silhouette of the object. If there are edge loops in the geometry that do not add anything to the shape, they are not necessary, as shown in Figure 3-2. The mesh on the left has extra edge loops, while the mesh on the right keeps an optimized low poly count.

***Figure 3-2.*** *Meshes showing correct and incorrect amount of edge loops*

# Exception to the Rule

There are times where additional edge loops will be used. This is where knowledge of animation and rigging is helpful. For instance, a character's hand would have more edge loops (see Figure 3-3) around its wrist so the hand can move properly. The edges are not affecting the form of the hand, but rather its movement. For this reason, modelers don't always know exactly how much geometry will be needed in certain areas as desired by an animator. This is why we refer to the 3D pipeline as nonlinear. The communication and production between the modeler, animator, and rigger will go back and forth until their goals are achieved.

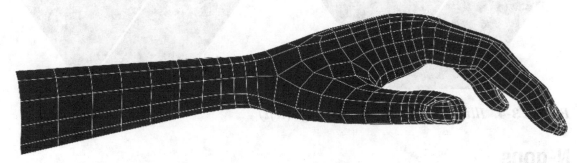

***Figure 3-3.*** *Topology shown in a model of a hand*

# Topology

The distribution and placement of edges that define the form of the mesh is known as *topology*. Beyond keeping the base mesh at a low poly count, there are some topology guidelines you need to follow in order to avoid issues further along in the pipeline. Unclean topology can cause issues specifically related to texturing and rendering, as well as for models that will deform for animation.

The issues that need to be considered within our edges are more numerous than can be covered in this book, therefore I cover two that are the most important. Although there are exceptions to the rule, edges should travel all around the surface uninterrupted, creating a complete edge loop. Figure 3-4 shows an example of an incomplete edge loop, where an edge is missing. The image on the right has a complete edge loop.

***Figure 3-4.*** *Illustration of a missing edge (left)*

# N-gons

A mesh should not have a face with more than four edges. This is known as an N-gon. Figure 3-5 shows an example of an N-gon. The image on the left has clean topology and the one on the right shows one of the faces with 56 edges.

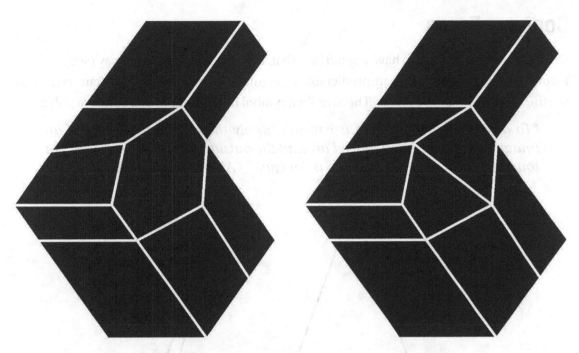

***Figure 3-5.*** *Illustration of N-gons in topology*

N-gons can lead to a wide range of problems. Without getting too in-depth into this topic, one solution for fixing N-gons is by means of *triangulation*—the process by which an N-gon gets subdivided into triangles. At runtime for game engines, all faces go through the process of triangulation.

Technically, every quad face is made up of two triangles (Figure 3-6). As the amount of sides increases, so does the amount of triangles it splits into. Therefore, it could become more difficult to render programs that handle 20 sides. This could lead to unpredictable results.

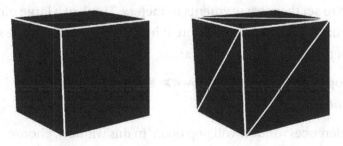

***Figure 3-6.*** *Illustration of a cube and triangulated cube*

# Concave Faces

On the other hand, you can have a quad face that, if exaggerated a certain way (see Figure 3-7), could also lead to unpredictable triangulation. Concave faces are curved in and are the opposite of convex faces. The Star Trek symbol is an example of a concave polygon.

*"To determine if a polygon is concave, apply the rubber band test. If an imaginary rubber band placed around the outside of a polygon would not touch all sides, then the polygon is concave." - Autodesk Maya 2010\**

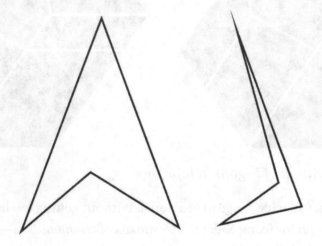

***Figure 3-7.*** *Illustration of concave faces*

# Metrics

At first, it may be confusing to understand that in an empty 3D space there is a metric system that needs to be utilized. By default (from the time of writing this book), Maya is set to measure in centimeters. As games have assets with real-life measurements, it is common practice to set the measurements to meters. Think of a large environment in real life. It might make less sense to measure it in centimeters and more sense to do so in meters. You can set your metrics as follows:

1. In the top menu, choose Windows ➤ Setting/Preferences ➤ Preferences.

2. The Preferences window will pop open. In this window, choose Settings. Settings will include the Linear dropdown menu, which should be switched to Meter. Then, you can close out of this window.

To make it easier to model in relation to a scale that you are familiar with, you will create a cube with human proportions.

3.  In the top menu, choose Create ➤ Polygon Primitives ➤ Cube.

4.  With the cube selected, in the Channel Box window, change the Scale X and Scale Z to 0.4 and Scale Y to 1.8, as shown in Figure 3-8.

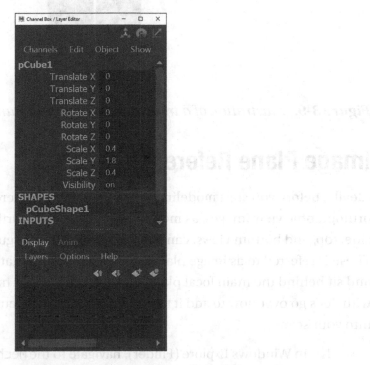

***Figure 3-8.*** *Screenshot of the Channel Box for creating the metric*

You can now use this cube as the metric for the mech.

*Figure 3-9.* *Illustration of a transformed cube with human proportions*

# Image Plane Reference

Ideally, before you start modeling, you should have gathered your references and orthographic view images, as mentioned in Chapter 1. Orthographic images such as side, top, and bottom views, can be used as background guidelines for the base mesh. These is referred to as image planes, which are planes that contain a projected image and sit behind the main focal plane in your scene. If you have your side image to start with, let's go over how to add it to the project folder structure so you can then bring it into your scene.

1. In Windows Explore (Finder), navigate to the Mech project folder you created in Chapter 2.

2. Inside this Mech folder you can copy and paste the images folder that came with this book's project files for Chapter 2.

3. Go back to Maya and, in the top menu, choose File ➤ Set Project.

4. Navigate to your Mech folder from Step 1 and Click Set.

Now that you have your images and project set for the chapter, let's import the side orthographic image into the scene as an image plane. By default, you are viewing from a perspective View Panel. Let's switch to the side view:

5.  In the top-left of the View Panel (the toolbar above the View Panel), choose Panels ➤ Orthographic ➤ Side.

6.  In the top left of the side View Panel toolbar, choose the Image Plane icon .

The Explorer or Finder Window will pop open. If you set your project correctly, the Mech folder should have opened, and you should see your Images folder as well as the rest of the project folders you created.

7.  Double-click to open the Images folder.

8.  Select your side ortho image, labeled ortho_side_left, and click Open.

Once your image successfully imports as an image plane, you can adjust its scale and position to be more aligned with how you need it.

In this case, let's make the mech in the side ortho image plane approximately double the height of the human metric.

9.  With the image plane selected:

    a.  Press R (scale tool)

    b.  Select and drag-select the center of the manipulator handle to scale it up.

---

**Tip**    You can double-click the imagePlane1 name in the Channel Box to rename it. We can add a suffix of _side_ortho to be more specific.

---

Now, you need to switch to perspective view to see it in relation to the 3D space:

1.  In the top-left of the View Panel (the toolbar above the View Panel), choose Panels ➤ Orthographic ➤ Perspective. See Figure 3-10.

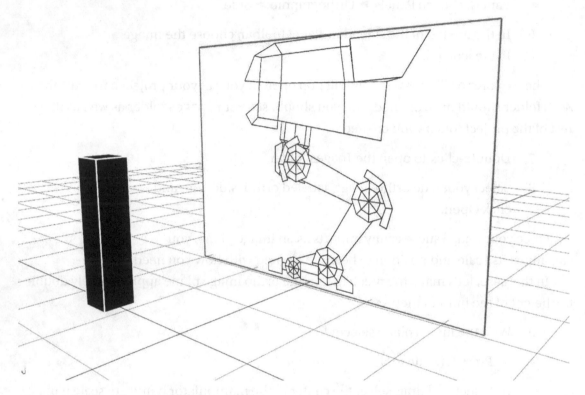

***Figure 3-10.***  *Illustration of Image Plane next to a metric*

Now that we have the Image Plane showing in the view panels and sitting behind the X axis, you can also hide it in specific view panels. To hide the Image Plane in a view panel, go to the View Panel toolbar and choose Show and then disable Image Planes.

# Switching Between Panel Views

You can also go to Quick Layout (see Figure 3-11) in order to change from one panel layout to another. such as the four panes that consist of the perspective, top, front, and side views, or two panes side by side. If you need to review the Quick Layout, refer back to Chapter 1. See Figure 3-12.

*Figure 3-11.* *Quick Layout menu*

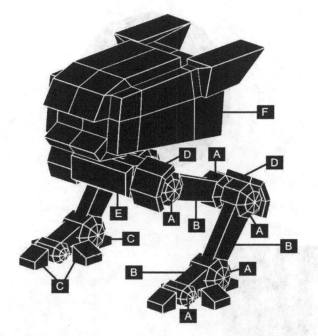

| A | MOTOR UNIT |
| B | LEG CONNECTOR |
| C | FOOT STABILIZER |
| D | MOTOR ARMOR |
| E | BODY |
| F | HEAD |

*Figure 3-12.* *Final mech model and part diagram*

# Starting to Model

The mech will be composed of motor units—leg connectors, foot stabilizers, motor armor, a body, and a head. Start by blocking out the model by creating the overall shapes and then adding the small details. Let's start by modeling the motor units (A) as follows:

1. In the top menu, choose Create ➤ Polygon Primitives ➤ Sphere.

2. Select the sphere.

It is easier to model with as little geometry as possible (Figure 3-13), so let's reduce the poly count in the following steps:

3.   With the sphere selected, in the Channel Box (see Figure 3-15), under the Inputs section, select polySphere1. This will open the polySphere1 settings.

4.   Change Subdivisions Axis to 8 and Subdivisions Height to 5.

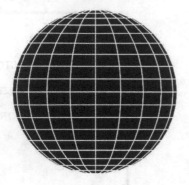 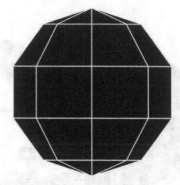

***Figure 3-13.***   *Sphere creation*

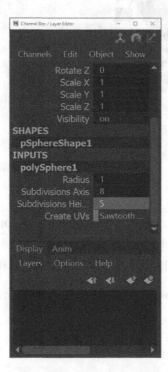

***Figure 3-14.***   *Screenshot of Channel box for the sphere*

# Symmetry

Now let's modify the shape of the sphere. By default, any edits you make to the mesh will only affect one side. Chapter 2 discussed methods of mirroring geometry, and you can also opt for another method of symmetrical editing. In order to be able to edit the top and bottom of the sphere simultaneously, you have to activate symmetry as follows:

1. Navigate to the status line and choose Symmetry from the dropdown menu (see Figure 3-15), which should be set to Symmetry: Off by default.

2. Choose World Y (see Figure 3-16).

The menu will show World Y highlighted in blue after enabled (see Figure 3-17).

***Figure 3-15.*** *Symmetry section within the status line*

***Figure 3-16.*** *Symmetry dropdown with World Y selected*

***Figure 3-17.*** *Symmetry changed to World Y*

Now, any changes you make to the top of the sphere will reflect to the bottom and vice versa. In the following steps, you will add details to shape the motor unit:

1.  Select the sphere in the previous steps.

2.  Right-click the sphere and drag-select over Vertex Mode in the Marking menu (if you need a refresher on the different component modes, refer to Chapter 2).

3.  While in Vertex Mode, drag-select the vertices you want to move from either the top or bottom (since symmetry is enabled).

    When you drag-select as opposed to simply selecting the vertices, you also select the ones directly behind them.

4.  With vertices selected, press W (the Translate tool).

5.  Position the vertices as illustrated in Figure 3-18. If it helps to see or select the correct vertices from the side, switch to the side view.

## Deselecting and Inverting Components

To deselect components (vertices, faces, and edges), hold Ctrl and click them. Drag-selecting while holding Ctrl will deselect the selection. To invert the selection of components, hold Shift and click them. Also, drag-selecting while holding Shift will invert the selection.

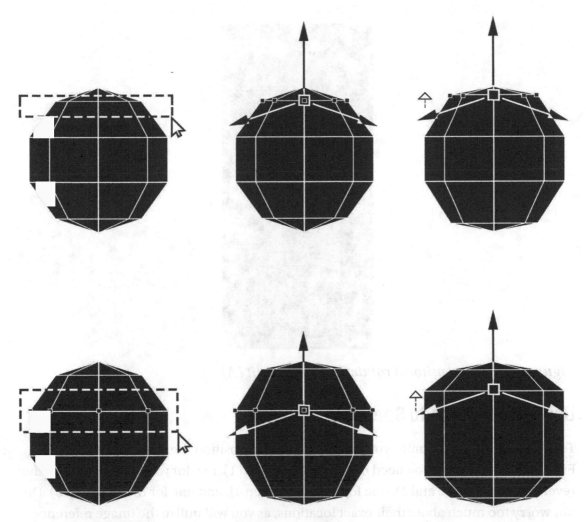

*Figure 3-18.* *Illustrations of Steps 1-6 of modeling a sphere into a motor unit (A)*

## Using the Channel Box for Transformation

The motor units (A) will need to be combined with the leg connectors (B), so they should be rotated. You can use the Channel Box to transform the sphere as follows:

1.  With the sphere selected, change Rotate Z to -90 (see Figure 3-19).

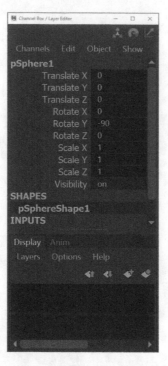

***Figure 3-19.*** *Screenshot of rotate Z of motor unit (A)*

# Using Duplicates to Speed Up Modeling

To create all the motor units, you can duplicate and position them as shown in Figures 3-20 and 3-21. You need one for the hip (Step 1), two for what you could call the reverse-knee (Steps 2 and 3), one for the ankle (Step 4), and one for the toe (Step 5). Do not worry too much about their exact locations, as you will utilize the image reference after. For now, you can use the metric cube you made at the beginning of the chapter and as shown in Figure 3-20.

1. Select the sphere you made previously.

2. Duplicate (Ctrl+D) and translate motors 1-4 and scale the 5th to end up as shown in Figures 3-20 and 3-21.

These will be the motor units for the mech, which will serve as joints.

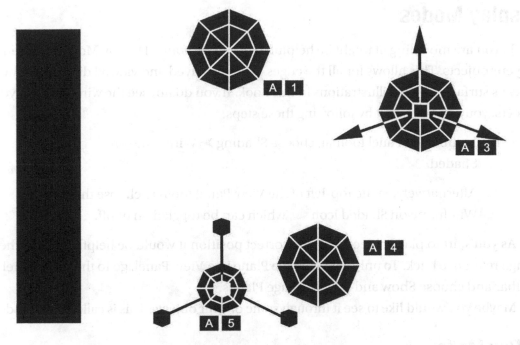

*Figure 3-20.* *Side view illustration of duplicated and scaled spheres*

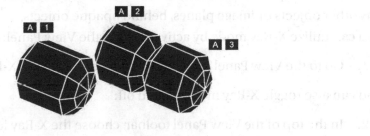

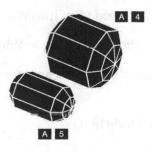

*Figure 3-21.* *Perspective view illustration of duplicated and scaled motor units (A)*

# Display Modes

While you are modeling, it might be helpful to have Wireframe Display Mode activated on your objects. This allows for all the edges to be displayed and viewed directly on the object's surface, like the illustrations in this book. If you do not see the wireframe on your objects, you can activate it by following these steps:

1. In the View Panel toolbar, choose Shading ➤ Wireframe on Shaded.

2. Alternatively, in the top-left of the View Panel toolbar, choose the Wireframe on Shaded icon ⬡, which can be toggled on or off.

As you start to place objects into the correct position it would be helpful to have the image reference back. To unhide the Image Plane in a View Panel, go to the View Panel toolbar and choose Show and Enable Image Planes.

Maybe you would like to see it through some of your objects. This is called Xray mode.

# X-Ray Mode

X-Ray Mode is a display mode that gives you the ability to slightly see and select things, such as other objects or image planes, behind opaque objects.

You can utilize X-Ray mode by activating it in the View Panel:

1. Go to the View Panel toolbar and choose Shading ➤ X-Ray.

You can also toggle X-Ray mode on and off:

2. In the top of the View Panel toolbar, choose the X-Ray icon. ⬒

Sometimes X-Ray Mode is not enough and it is even more beneficial to be able to see the wireframe on its own. For this, you need to go into Wireframe Mode.

1. In the View Panel toolbar, choose Shading ➤ Wireframe.

2. Alternatively, in the top left of the View Panel toolbar, choose the Wireframe icon. ⬡

3. Or press 4, the Wireframe Mode hotkey.

4.  In order to get out of Wireframe Mode and return to Shaded mode, in the top left of the side View Panel toolbar, choose the Smooth Shade All icon. 🔲

5.  Or press 5, the Smooth Shade All hotkey, to go back to smooth shaded mode.

Throughout this chapter and beyond this book, you might find that while you model you will constantly switch between the different display modes discussed. This is common among modelers, as seeing your models displayed in different modes helps you gain a better understanding of your model and all of its components at any given moment.

As you progress through the following steps to model the mech, you could make any necessary adjustments of the parts' positions to align with the image plane side guide you set up.

## Modeling the Leg Connectors

Now, you can create your leg connectors (B), which will serve as links between the motor units (A) using Figure 3-22.

1.  In the top menu, choose Create ➤ Polygon Primitives ➤ Cube.

2.  Select the cube (Figure 3-22, Step 1).

3.  Go to Perspective View.

4.  Make sure you are in Object Mode and scale the cube in the X axis, as shown in Figure 3-22, Step 2.

5.  Go to Side View.

6.  With the cube selected, go to Vertex Mode (right-click the cube and drag-select over Vertex Mode in the Marking menu).

Figure 3-22 shows how the first leg connector will appear in X-Ray Mode. Continue reading to create this leg connector.

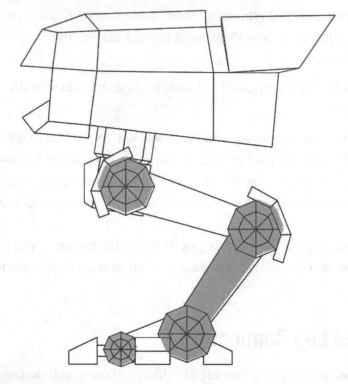

**Figure 3-22.**  *Leg in X-Ray mode with side ortho image plane sitting behind*

7.  Turn on X-Ray mode (choose Shading ➤ X-Ray) if it is not on already for the purpose of matching the leg connectors to the image plane.

8.  Select the vertices (see Figure 3-23, Step 3) or drag-select multiple vertices.

9.  Using the translate tool (W), move the selected vertices by using the arrows that appear on the manipulator handle (see Figures 3-23 and 3-24). Each arrow corresponds to the, X, Y, or Z axis.

Selecting one arrow will move vertices in one axis, while selecting the middle box will move vertices in more than one axis at a time.

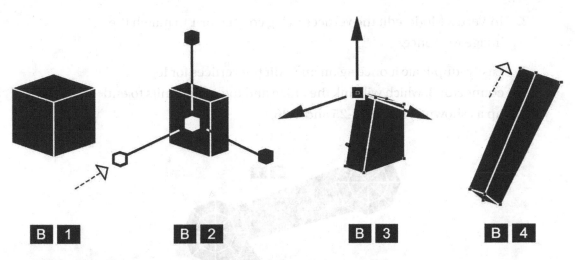

**Figure 3-23.** *Turning the cube into the leg connector (B)*

**Figure 3-24.** *The leg connector's (B) vertices*

## Duplicating the Shapes of the Leg Connectors

1.  Duplicate (Ctrl+D) and move (W) the leg connector 2 that you previously made to make the leg connector 1, as shown in Figures 3-25 and 3-26.

    This will link the hip and knee motor units (A).

2.  In Vertex Mode, edit the vertices of leg connector 1 to match the image reference.

3.  Lastly, duplicate it once again and edit the vertices for leg connector 3, which will link the ankle and toe motor units to end up as shown in Figures 3-25 and 3-26.

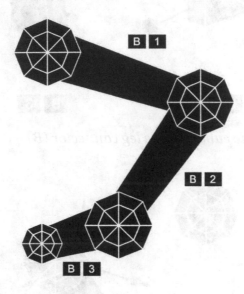

***Figure 3-25.***  *Illustration of leg connectors*

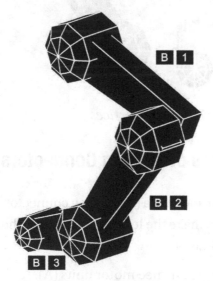

***Figure 3-26.***  *Illustration of leg connectors in perspective view*

I only cover the modeling of the basic shapes and simpler forms for the mech in this book. However, these shapes are provisional and can certainly be refined and be more detailed. For instance, some of these forms may be more real-life and could interlock with one another to provide movement as a hinge, coupling, or other joint mechanism.

## Modeling the Foot Stabilizers

Now, you can create foot stabilizers (C) (see Figure 3-27), which will act like the toes for the mech. You need one for the front, back, left, and right side of the mech's foot.

1.  In the top menu, choose Create ➤ Polygon Primitives ➤ Cube.

2.  Select the cube.

    Continue to use Figure 3-27 to achieve the following steps:

3.  Right-click the cube and change to Edge Mode.

4.  Select the appropriate edge(s).

5.  Using the translate tool (W) and arrows on the manipulator handle, move the edge down.

Next, you'll work on applying more topology to the mesh to begin shaping it. Continue to refer to Figure 3-27. If you miss any of the steps, you can use Ctrl+Z to undo.

6.  Right-click the cube and change to Face Mode.

7.  Select the side face of Step 3.

8.  Press R to enter into the Scale tool.

9.  With the face still selected, hold Shift and drag-select middle cube (of scale manipulator) to extrude the face inward, as shown in Step 5 of Figure 3-27.

10. Then, press Ctrl+E (the other extrude method) to move it outward to the end, as shown in Step 6.

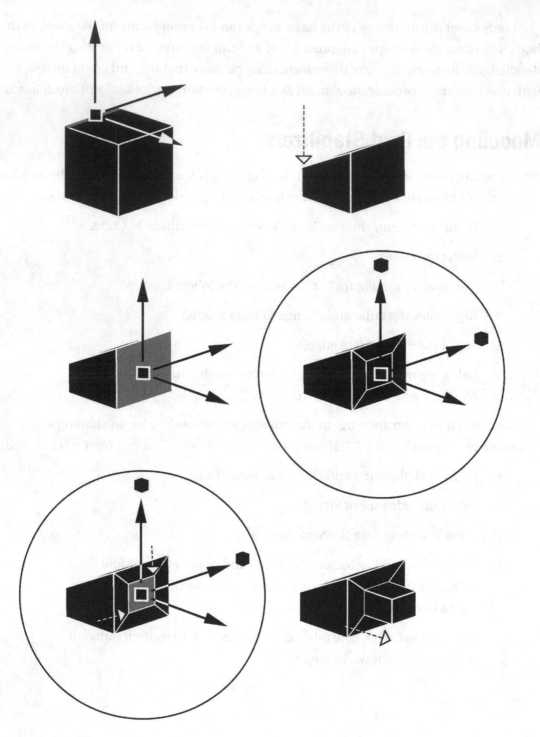

**Figure 3-27.** *Illustrations of Steps 1-6 of modeling a cube into a foot stabilizer (C)*

Next, position the foot stabilizers (C) as they are in Figure 3-28:

11. In Object Mode, choose the foot stabilizer (C) you made in the previous section and position it in one of the locations illustrated in Figure 3-28.

12. Then, with the foot stabilizer still selected, duplicate (Ctrl+D), translate (W), and rotate (E) as needed.

13. Repeat Step 2 two more times (see Figure 3-28).

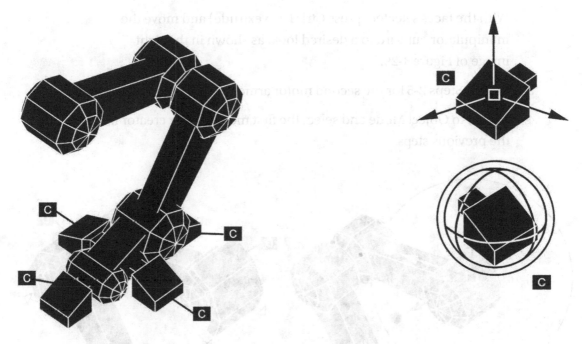

**Figure 3-28.** *Illustration of foot stabilizers in place*

## Modeling Armor for the Motor Units

Next, let's create armor-looking shapes that wrap around the joints of the leg. Use Figure 3-29 for reference when following these steps:

1. Right-click the hip motor unit and change to Face Mode,

2. Hold Shift and select the faces, as shown in the left image in Figure 3-29.

3. Then, in the top menu, choose Edit Mesh ➤ Duplicate and transform outward using the manipulator arrows.

After duplicating and moving these faces outward, they will be detached from the motor units with a gap between each other. At this point, the armor should be looking pretty thin. Let's thicken it up.

1. Hold Shift and select the faces of the newly detached armor shapes. Alternatively, you can quickly select all the faces or components of an entire mesh by double-clicking one of the faces.

2. With the faces selected, press Ctrl+E (to extrude) and move the manipulator outward to a desired look, as shown in the right image of Figure 3-29.

3. Repeat Steps 2-5 for the second motor armor.

4. Switch to Object Mode and select the first motor armor creator in the previous steps.

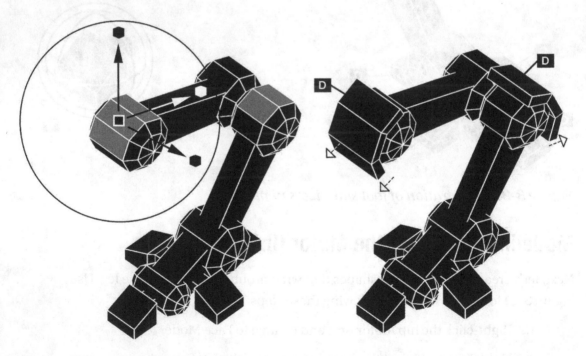

***Figure 3-29.*** *Illustration of armor creation for the motor unit*

5.  With the armor selected, press W and transform it to touch the motor units, as shown in Figure 3-30.

6.  Repeat the last step for the second motor armor.

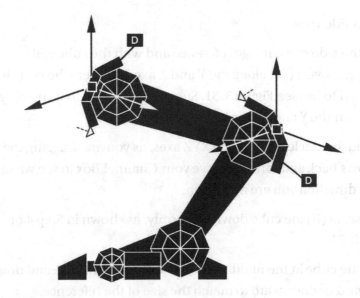

***Figure 3-30.*** *Illustration of Motor Armor placement*

# Building the Body

The mech needs a body that connects to the legs and head. Since the body should be able to turn without moving the legs, you will create separate structures to lie in between both.

1.  Let's use a cube to make the body (E). From the top menu, choose Create ➤ Polygon Primitives ➤ Cube.

2.  Go into perspective view.

3.  With the cube selected, press R to switch to Scale Mode and scale the cube following the steps shown in Figure 3-31.

4.  Scale the cube along the X axis to elongate the cube into a rectangular shape, as shown in Figure 3-31, Step 2.

When this cube for the body was created, it originated in the center. Let's keep it in the center since the mech needs to be centered in the middle of the grid. You will also use Uniform Scaling, which is enlarging or shrinking an object by a scale factor that is the same amount in all directions or along all axes.

5.  Go into side view.

6.  Using the side ortho image reference and with the cube still selected, move it (W) along the Y and Z axes to where the body is supposed to be (see Figure 3-31, Step 3). Make sure that you only move it on the Y and Z axes.

    a.  If you are unclear about the XYZ axes, as you are dragging the arrows back and forth, observe your Channel Box to see which axis and direction you are moving in.

7.  Then, scale (R) the cube down uniformly, as shown in Step 4 of Figure 3-31.

8.  Select the cube in the middle of the manipulator handle and drag it outward or downward to match the size of the reference.

Do not worry about the leg's location while you work on the body, as it is covered at the end of this chapter.

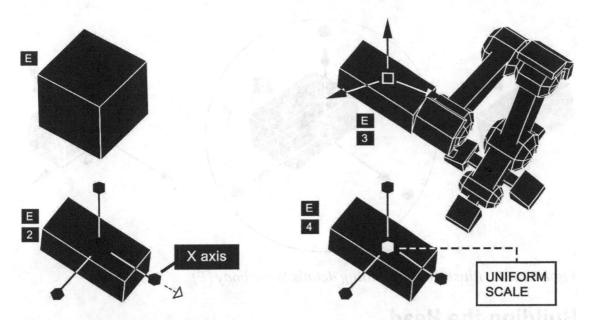

***Figure 3-31.*** *Illustration of Steps 1-4 of modeling the body (E) from a cube and positioning it next to the leg model*

## Adding Details to the Body

1. Right-click the body and change to Face Mode. Then, select the front face and extrude (Ctrl+E) it outward, as shown in Figure 3-32.

2. Right-click the body and change to Edge Mode. Make the following modifications to end up as shown in the last image of Figure 3-32:

   a. Select the top front edge and move (W) it down slightly.

   b. Select the bottom-front edge and move it in and up slightly.

   c. You can refine the shape by referencing the image plane in the side view.

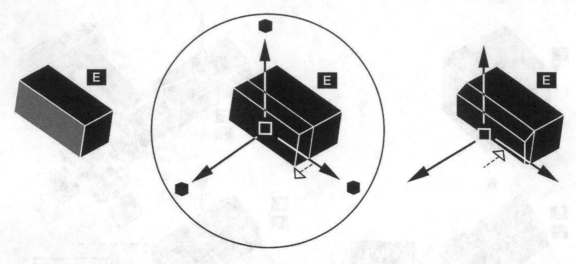

*Figure 3-32.*  *Illustration of adding details to the body (E)*

# Building the Head

As you build the head of the mech, you need to keep in mind its functionality. Since you are thinking ahead about whether you'll need to rig this object or are working with someone else that will do so, you will keep the mesh separated. This head needs to be able to rotate side to side.

1. Let's use another cube to make this head (F). In the top menu, choose Create ➤ Polygon Primitives ➤ Cube.

2. If the cube is not already selected, click it and scale (R) it up in Z axis to the size shown in Figure 3-33.

3. Switch to side view and move (W) it into position to align with the side ortho image plane. It should be somewhat floating above the body mesh.

4. Rotate (E) the head so it is angled upward, as shown in the last step of Figure 3-33.

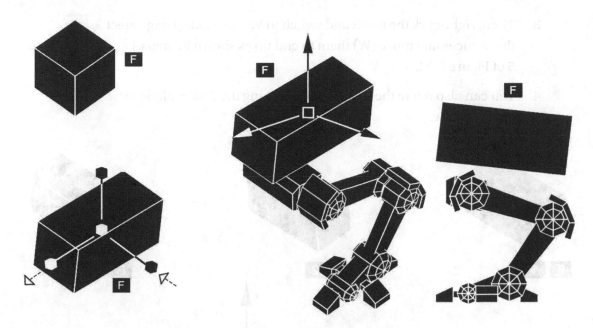

*Figure 3-33.* *Illustration of steps to create the head (F) from a cube*

# Shaping the Head

To be able to shape the head, you need further topology for it. Let's add edge loops to the mesh.

1. With the head (F) selected, choose Mesh Tools ➤ Multi-Cut in the top menu.

2. While in the Multi-Cut tool, hold Ctrl and move your cursor across the surface (without clicking) to preview the edge loop.

   a. While still holding Ctrl, click to add an edge loop along the mesh length, near the front of the mesh. Add another one near the back of the mesh in the locations illustrated as dotted lines in Step 2 of Figure 3-34.

   b. Continue to hold Ctrl and click once more along the height of the mesh to add an edge loop, as shown as in the dotted line in Step 3 of Figure 3-34.

3.  Then, right-click the mesh and switch to Vertex Mode. Drag-select the vertices and move (W) them to end up as shown in Steps 4 and 5 of Figure 3-34.

4.  You can also refine the shape by referencing the image plane in the side view.

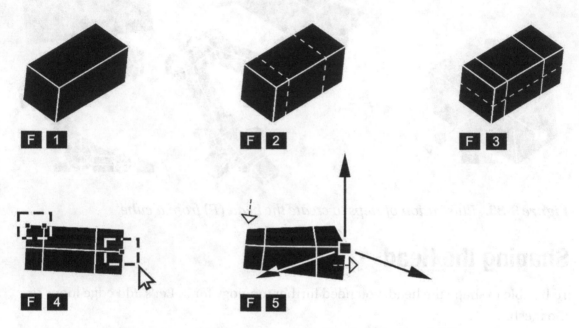

*Figure 3-34.* *Illustration of Steps 1-5, further shaping the head (F)*

# Adding Thickness to the Head

The main head is looking small in comparison to the leg and body. Let's bulk it up!

1.  With the head (F) selected, go to Face Mode.

2.  Hold Shift and select the outer faces of both sides of the mesh (or use the symmetry method from previous steps), as shown in Step 1 of Figure 3-35. Then, extrude (Ctrl+E) them outward a bit to end up as illustrated in Step 2 of Figure 3-35.

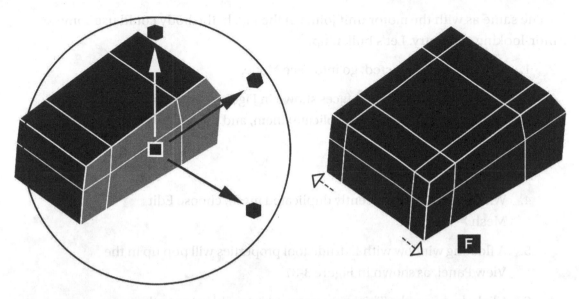

**Figure 3-35.** *Illustration of the sides of the head (F) being extruded*

# Modeling the Head Details

Before you start adding more geometry, you can add a centerline, which will be an edge loop that runs directly down the middle of the model from the front view. This will help you later, when positioning your model on the center of the X axis on the grid, so that the model is symmetrical on both sides.

1. Select the head mesh (F).

2. For the first step of Figure 3-36, use the Multi-Cut (Mesh Tools ➤ Multi-Cut) tool technique once again to add an edge loop that runs down the center of the head mesh.

   a. With the Multi-Cut tool selected, press and hold Ctrl+Shift, which will snap the preview edge loops as you move across the surface.

   b. Add one edge loop in the location illustrated in Step 1 of Figure 3-36. This will be the model's center line.

The same as with the motor unit joints of the mech, the body could use some armor-looking geometry. Let's bulk it up!

1. With the head selected, go into Face Mode.

2. Hold Shift and select the faces shown in Figure 3-36, Step 2. Duplicate (Edit Mesh ➤ Duplicate) them, and this time do not move them.

3. Go back to Object Mode.

4. While selecting the recently duplicated mesh, choose Edit Mesh ➤ Extrude.

5. A floating window with Extrude tool properties will pop up in the View Panel, as shown in Figure 3-37.

6. Click-drag over the Thickness parameter to add value to the thickness of the mesh. This value may differ slightly from scene to scene, so refer to Figure 3-36, Step 3 or the side ortho image plane for best reference.

7. Go to Edge Mode.

8. Select the front top edges and move (W) them downward and inward to a desired look, as shown in Figure 3-36, Step 4.

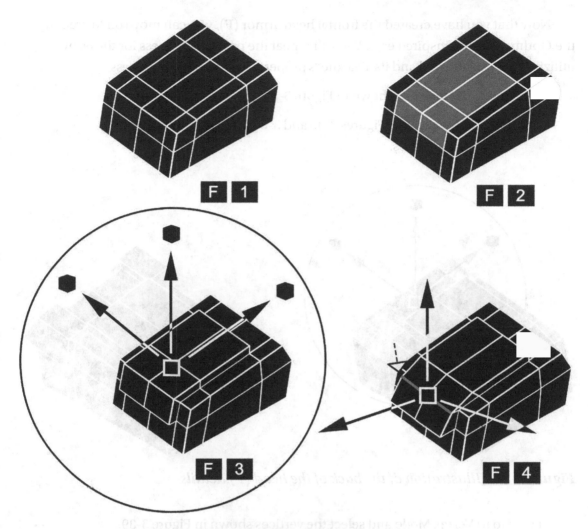

**Figure 3-36.**  *The head's (F) front detail modeling process*

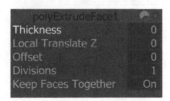

**Figure 3-37.**  *Screenshot of Extrude tool properties*

Now that you have created the frontal head armor (F), you can move on to creating the Optimus-Prime inspired ears. You will repeat the previous process for these, by utilizing the Extrude tool and its Thickness property to introduce thickness.

9.    Select the faces, as shown in Figure 3-38.

10.    Refer to the steps in Figures 3-36 and 3-37 for duplicating and extruding the faces.

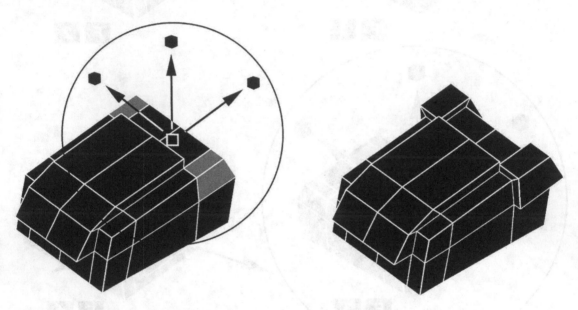

*Figure 3-38.* *Illustration of the back of the head (F) details*

11.    Go to Vertex Mode and select the vertices shown in Figure 3-39. Move them backward and outward to the desired look.

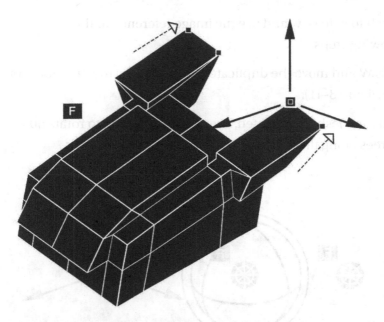

**Figure 3-39.** *Illustration of the back of the head (F) vertices details*

12. Once again, repeat the previous process to create the chin armor for the head (F), as shown in Figure 3-40.

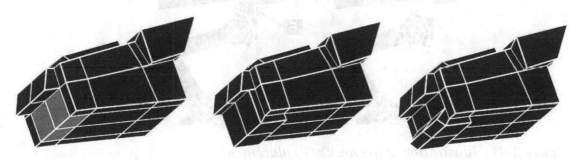

**Figure 3-40.** *Illustration of the front bottom of the head (F) details*

# Adding the Neck Model

Finally, since the head is floating over the body, you need to create a neck. To do this, you can utilize existing geometry in the following steps:

1. Select the motor unit that is closer to the body. Then, press Ctrl+D to duplicate it.

2. Switch to side view and use the image reference in the following steps.

3. Press W and move the duplicated motor unit to the neck location (see Figure 3-41).

4. With the mesh still selected, use the Channel Box to rotate 90 degrees along the Z axis.

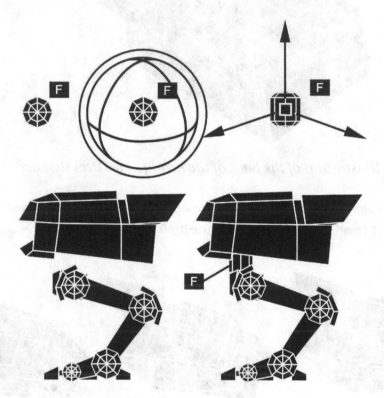

***Figure 3-41.*** *Illustration of the neck's (F) placement*

## Positioning the Leg

The left leg components (which consists of motor units, leg connectors, foot stabilizers, and motor armor) need to be grouped together to make it easy to move it as a whole. We cover this more in Chapter 4, when we discuss grouping within the Outliner. For now, you can group it as follows:

1. Hold Shift and select all the motor units, leg connectors, foot stabilizers, and motor armor. Then, press Ctrl+G to group them.

2.  With the group selected, move the leg to the side of the body, as illustrated in the previous steps. Make sure the body is centered and does not get selected and moved during this process.

---

**Tip**    If you select an object within a group and press the up arrow on the keyboard, its entire group will be selected.

---

# Instancing the Leg

Now that you have grouped the leg and positioned it, mirror the leg across the X axis using the Duplicate Special Instance method.

First, you need to consider the pivot's offset, then instance the geometry. When you first grouped the objects together, by default the group's pivot point is automatically set to the center. However, the pivot point may have shifted when you positioned the leg. Any offset in the X axis, in this case, will essentially create an offset in the mirrored object.

Follow these steps to relocate the group's pivot point back to the center of the grid:

1.  With the leg group selected, go to the move tool (W).

2.  Press D (Edit Pivot mode).

3.  While holding X, left-click and drag the center of the manipulator handle to the center of the grid, ensuring it snaps to the center grid lines.

Instancing geometry links the original and the copied versions. This allows you to make additional changes to the mirrored object that will automatically update on the original object and vice versa. Refer to Chapter 2 to review the other mirroring geometry methods and the Duplicate Special types.

4.  Set up the Duplicate Special Instance as shown in Figure 3-42:

    a.  In the top menu, choose Edit ➤ Duplicate Special ➤ Options box.

    b.  Change Geometry type to Instance.

c.  Then, Scale should be set to -1(x), 1(y), and 1(z).

d.  Select Duplicate Special.

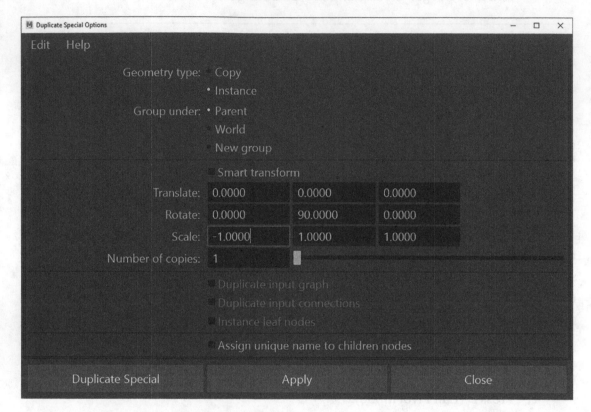

*Figure 3-42.* *Duplicate Special Options popup window*

The left leg should now be duplicated to the other side of the body, as shown in Figure 3-43. If there is any offset in the leg or if it was duplicated in the wrong transform, repeat the previous steps until both legs are equidistant from the center grid line.

***Figure 3-43.*** *Final mech model with right leg instanced and mirrored to the other side of the body*

## Summary

In this chapter, you started creating a mech model, thinking about how your choices will affect things further along the pipeline. You started to apply basic modeling techniques that were introduced in Chapter 2. You began the workflow of modeling an entire object. The chapter also briefly discussed the guidelines for topology and poly count. Finally, the chapter ended with a block-out of the mech project.

# CHAPTER 4

# Preparing the Asset for the Next Phase

Up to this point, you have mainly worked on the different aspects of the asset pipeline without looking ahead. Since you need to think about how all these chapters will lead to the production of one asset, this chapter focuses on making sure the mech is properly set up for the next steps. This chapter covers the pipeline's best practices, using the Outliner, cleaning up the scene, naming conventions, modifying transforms, and optimizing pivot locations.

## Adopting Best Practices

During the model-creation process within a pipeline, particularly in game development, it is common for multiple artists, technical artists, technical animators, designers, animators, programmers, and so forth to work on the same Maya scene. In other words, your current scene will most likely be handled by people other than you after you hand it off to the next stage of the pipeline, and they will need to be able to navigate the scene with as much ease as possible. Therefore, it is crucial, when starting out, to develop best practices.

## Pipeline Requirements

From working alone to being a part of a game development team, you need to think about how the mech will be used at later stages within the pipeline. This includes rigging and the process of creating a high poly model (see Figure 4-1). To accomplish this, you can start by organizing your scene files.

© Nova Villanueva 2022
N. Villanueva, *Beginning 3D Game Assets Development Pipeline*,
https://doi.org/10.1007/978-1-4842-7196-4_4

*Figure 4-1.* *Flowchart of the preparation stages*

It is common practice to use naming conventions for organization. You need to think further than the one asset you are currently creating. After all, this asset is meant to be a part of a game that holds many assets. As there could be thousands of assets in a game, some kind of naming system is recommended. The industry has certain naming conventions utilized across teams for everyone to be able to access anything they need to work on. There is no one proper way to name assets, as different game development studios each have their own approach. However, it is important to have a system that is clear, cohesive, and that a team can stick with for the length of the project. For example, efficiently naming a prop asset (see Figure 4-2) as `prop_small_bear_01`.

*Figure 4-2.* *Illustration of a wireframe 3D teddy bear prop*

Let's start by cleaning up the scene. In the following steps, you can continue from the final work completed in Chapter 3 or open the starting file, named `start_ch4`.

# What Is the Outliner and Why Do You Use It?

The Outliner consists of all the objects within the scene, including 3D models, cameras, and lights. All the objects are listed in a hierarchical form like an outline. The objects are organized with expandable and collapsible branches. For example, a group of objects can be one branch with sublevels.

The Outliner usage can include naming, selecting, grouping, and deleting objects. Having all of the scene's objects organized within this window is essential to game development pipelines. Maya defaults to object naming without any conventions and therefore it is up to the users to edit and arrange them.

It is common for beginners to not organize the Outliner while working in Maya. However, the more you use Maya, the more you will realize its benefits. Some objects can easily be selectable within the scene, but this is not always the case for all objects.

There are some objects that show up in the Outliner that are not visible in the 3D view. Hence, it is important to understand the strengths of the View and Outliner panels alongside each other and not as a replacement. 3D artists are constantly using the Outliner. Therefore, as you have used the View Panel throughout Chapter 3, this chapter mainly covers the Outliner.

First, let's open the Outliner so you can look at it:

1. If the Outliner window (see Figure 4-3) is not already open, choose Windows ➤ Outliner. in the top menu.

***Figure 4-3.*** *The Outliner window*

Table 4-1 shows the basics of how to use the Outliner.

***Table 4-1.*** *Using the Outliner*

| Perform This Action | Results In |
| --- | --- |
| Click the node name. | Selecting an object. |
| Hold Shift/Ctrl+click the node names. | Selecting multiple objects. |
| Click the plus (expand) or minus (collapse) icons to the left of the nodes. | Expanding or collapsing nodes. |
| Select node with middle-mouse and hold-drag to another location. | Rearranging nodes. |
| Double-click the node name, type a new node name, and press Enter. | Renaming a node. |

# Using the Outliner for Clean Up

Without looking at the Outliner from all the steps in Chapters, you can predict that it is a mess. You can clean this up.

For this next part, your Outliner components may look different than what is shown in Figure 4-3. This is based on factors such as not having the exact same construction history or groupings when creating the mech, which can result in a differently arranged Outliner.

Just as you grouped the right leg in Chapter 3, grouping (Ctrl+G) is a way of gathering objects that you can then select and transform as a single unit. Groups are represented in the Outliner as expandable and collapsible nodes. Maya also keeps track of the objects' construction histories and transformation data and can create additional branches due to it. Let's briefly take a deeper dive into construction history and learn how to clean it up.

# What Is Construction History?

As you create, work on, and edit objects in Maya, most actions you do will convert to nodes that build on an object's construction history. This eventually creates a chain of nodes, and the construction history allows for changes to it. The transform attributes of these construction nodes can be edited in the Channel Box (where they are listed under Inputs).

The more operations you perform on your objects and in the scene, the more the construction history builds up. This could lead to a scene with a heavier file size and often leads to potentially corruptible nodes. Therefore, as a modeler, it is important that you keep your scenes optimized and maintained.

Furthermore, when construction history is not cleaned up, it could end up showing in the Outliner as empty branches.

# Cleaning Up the History

As mentioned, construction history can potentially start showing up in the Outliner as the undeleted history piles up. There are two types of actions within Maya to delete history: Delete All By Type History or Delete by Type History. It is important to understand their differences.

Deleting history through "Delete by Type" refers to deleting the history of the selected objects, while deleting history through "Delete All by Type" refers to deleting all history within the scene.

There are cases where it is crucial to choose the correct delete action. For example, when you learn more about 3D animation, files containing skin bind data need the history to be preserved for them to work. Therefore, in such scenarios, you could not use "Delete All By Type" in those scenes. With that said, if you are working within a scene that contains only static models, this is less of a concern.

Multiple modelers may be working on the same scene, but their construction history could look completely different—this is normal. This will show up when you don't have the exact number of objects or arrangement in the Outliner as another person. What will be important is that you both end up with the same clean scene file. Let's start to clean it up. Back in the top menu, choose Edit ➤ Delete all by type ➤ History.

To start out, we used "Delete All By Type," but for the rest of the deleting history actions in this chapter, you will stick with using "Delete By Type". A 3D artist should develop this habit.

## Starting to Use the Outliner

You are either working with the file you made in Chapter 3 or you can utilize start_ch4 provided by this book. In this file, you will notice in the Maya scene that the construction history cleanup for the mech has already been done for you.

As you continue the exercises, the Outliner is opened for the rest of this chapter. For changes that you make in the View panel (scene), you will notice them affecting the Outliner. For other steps, you can solely use the Outliner.

1. Make sure the Outliner is open or choose Windows ➤ Outliner in the top menu to open it.

2. In the Outliner, choose imagePlane1_side_ortho and press Ctrl+H (to hide it).

3. Back in the View panel, choose one item from the right leg and press the up arrow (to select the entire instance group). The Outliner should show one of the groups selected and highlighted in blue.

4.  With the group selected, press Delete. Afterwards, the Outliner should only show one group left, as shown in Figure 4-4. This one should contain the left leg components.

**Figure 4-4.** *Deleted group within the Outliner*

---

**Tip**    To unhide a hidden object node (displayed as faded text) in the Outliner, select it and press Shift+H.

---

5.  Still in the Outliner, choose the plus icon to the left of group1. This will expand the group containing the left leg, as shown in Figure 4-5.

**Figure 4-5.**  *Expanded left leg group1 object nodes*

6.  Then, with the group expanded, select all the object nodes within it, as shown in Figure 4-6.

Nodes nested under a group or other object nodes are commonly referred to as children of that group, while the group node is referred to as the parent node.

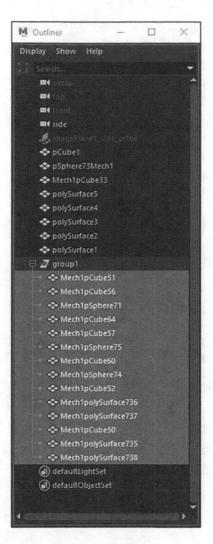

***Figure 4-6.*** *Selected left leg group object nodes*

7. With these object nodes still selected, press Shift+P to unparent
   them or remove them from their parent groups. This will leave the
   group and meshes separated in the Outliner, as shown in
   Figure 4-7.

**Figure 4-7.** *Unparented selected object nodes*

Essentially, you will be left with an empty group node without any children (see Figure 4-7). You no longer need this need node; therefore, you can go ahead and delete it.

Select the group node named group1 (it may have a different group number in your scene) and press Delete. See Figure 4-8

Finally, you should have an Outliner with all the object nodes and no groups left, as shown in Figure 4-9.

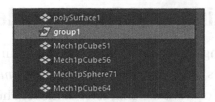

**Figure 4-8.** *The group node to delete*

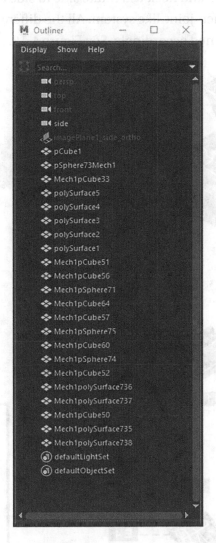

**Figure 4-9.** *Unparented selected object nodes*

# Combining, Naming, and Freezing Meshes

To set up the mech for rigging, which then can be used for animation; the rigger needs to think of how the mech needs to move first. The rigger or *technical animator* will usually have a say in how they need or want the character to move. Thus, the rigger works closely with the animator to understand all the rigging requirements.

For this project, the head and neck will rotate side to side and the leg will move like a human's with a reversed-knee-joint-like system. All the different components that must be moved need to be combined accordingly. See Figure 4-10.

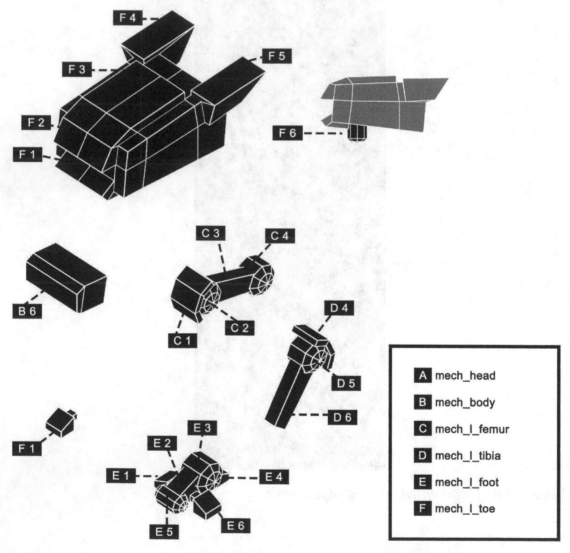

*Figure 4-10.*  *Diagram showing separated meshes of the mech*

1. Hold Shift and select all pieces from the upper leg (see Figure 4-11): first motor armor (C1), motor unit (C2), leg connector (C3), and last motor unit (C4). Then choose Mesh ➤ Combine.

2. With the mesh selected in the View Panel, choose Edit ➤ Delete by Type ➤ History from the top menu.

3. With the upper leg meshes still selected in the View Panel, the Outliner will show this combined mesh selected. Double-click it in the Outliner and name it mech_l_femur.

4. Hold Shift and select all the pieces from the bottom leg (see Figure 4-11): first motor armor (D5), motor unit (D6), and leg connector (D7). Then choose Mesh ➤ Combine.

5. With the mesh selected in the View Panel, press Alt/Option+Shift+D (or choose Edit ➤ Delete by Type ➤ History).

6. With the bottom leg meshes still selected in the View Panel, the Outliner will show this combined mesh selected. Double-click it in the Outliner and name it mech_l_tibia.

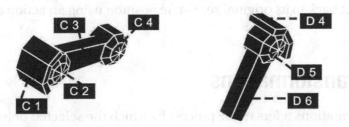

*Figure 4-11.*  *Diagram showing separated meshes of the mech's leg*

7. Hold Shift and select pieces from the foot (see Figure 4-12): motor units (E3 and E4), leg connector (E2); and foot stabilizers (E1, E5 and E6). Then choose Mesh ➤ Combine.

8. With the foot meshes selected in the View Panel, press Alt/Option+Shift+D (to delete history by type).

9. With the mesh still selected in the View Panel, the Outliner will show this combined mesh selected. Double-click it in the Outliner and name it mech_l_foot.

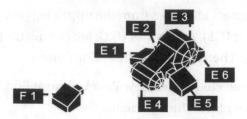

**Figure 4-12.** *Diagram showing separated meshes of the mech's foot*

Within Maya, an object's position information is stored in a transform node every time it is transformed (translated, rotated, or scaled). If at any time an object's transformation values need to be brought back to zero or set to a new starting position, the transforms can be reset or frozen. For example, when bringing the asset into a game engine, it needs to be in a zero-state position or frozen transforms. Without this, if a programmer makes a change to the position of the asset, it will be unclear which is its default position.

# Resetting Transformations

Resetting transformations refers to the process by which the selected object's current transforms are set back to its original zero-state position using an action called *reset transformations*.

# Freezing Transformations

Freezing transformations refers to the process by which the selected object's current transforms become the new original zero-state position, using an action called *freeze transformations*.

When you combine multiple objects into one object, as you have been doing, the transformations on all selected objects become frozen automatically as their position information becomes one. However, for single objects, you need to manually do this step. Let's keep this in mind as you work on the toe.

1. Select the toe mesh and choose Modify ➤ Freeze Transformation in the top menu.

2. With the toe mesh selected in the View Panel, press Alt/ Option+Shift+D (to delete history by type).

3.  With the toe mesh still selected in the View Panel, the Outliner will be selected. Double-click it in the Outliner and name it mech_1_toe.

4.  Hold Shift and select pieces F1 - F6 from the head, as shown in Figure 4-13. Then, choose Mesh ➤ Combine.

5.  With the head meshes selected in the View Panel, press Alt/ Option+Shift+D (to delete history by type).

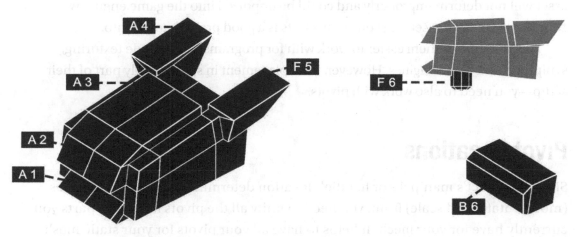

***Figure 4-13.*** *Select all these pieces*

6.  With the head mesh still selected in the View Panel, the Outliner will show this combined mesh selected. Double-click it in the Outliner and name it mech_head.

7.  Lastly, select the body, piece B6 (see Figure 4-13). Then, in the top menu, choose Modify ➤ Freeze Transformation.

8.  With the foot meshes selected in the View Panel, press Alt/ Option+Shift+D (to delete history by type).

9.  With the mesh still selected in the View Panel, the Outliner will show this combined mesh selected. Double-click it in the Outliner and name it mech_body.

Last, but not LEAST, let's name the metric that you created at the beginning of Chapter 3:

1. In the Outliner, double-click the metric mesh and name it `metric`.

2. Then, with the metric still selected, in the top menu, choose Modify ➤ Freeze Transformation.

Now, you have a cleaned-up scene that has combined the meshes, froze the transforms, and deleted the history. These steps are important as they ensure that your asset will not deform improperly and could be imported into the game engine with grid coordinates of 0,0,0. "Zeroing" out your assets is a good practice to get into.

This also makes them easier to work with for programs that include texturing, sculpting, and game engines. However, their placement in space is only part of their setup—you need to also work with pivots.

# Pivot Locations

Since an object's manipulator handle's location determines where it transforms (move, rotate, and scale) from, you need to unify all the pivots for all the parts you currently have for your mech. It helps to have all your pivots for your static meshes all the same spot. That way, centering all the pivots to the grid makes the scene cleaner and optimized, especially for others down the pipeline who need to work in this file. See Figure 4-14.

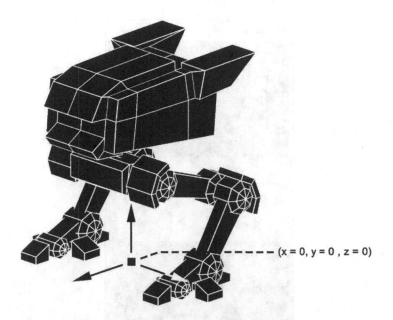

*(x = 0, y = 0 , z = 0)*

**Figure 4-14.** *Illustration of the mech at the origin of the grid*

Later in the rigging chapter, you will adjust the pivot according to your needs. For instance, the head should pivot from the location of the neck. However, in the meantime, let's center all of the mech parts' pivot points to the center of the grid. To do this, follow these steps:

1. In the Outliner, hold Ctrl and select all the meshes, as shown in Figure 4-15.

2. With the meshes selected, press W (the Move tool).

3. Press D (Edit Pivot mode).

4. While holding X, middle-mouse-click and drag from the center of the manipulator handle to the center of the grid (ensuring it snaps to the center grid lines).

*Figure 4-15.  Selected named meshes within the Outline*

# Using Instancing for Fast Prototyping

Just as you created an instance (special duplicate) of the leg for previewing the mech in the last chapter, you will do the same in this chapter. This is common in the industry. It's an ideal process, but it's only temporary until new changes are made that will require a new generated instance.

Originally, you had your mech's left leg grouped and then instanced to the right side. However, that instance was packed with unfrozen transforms and construction history. Now that you have optimized geometry, you can utilize the instancing geometry again for you new leg. As a refresher, this allows you to make additional changes to the mirrored object that will automatically update on the original object and vice versa. And finally, you can make the instance:

1. In the Outliner, hold Ctrl and select the mech_l_femur, mech_l_tibia, mech_l_foot, and mech_l_toe meshes.

2. Then, with the meshes selected, choose Edit ➤ Duplicate Special ➤ Options box in the top menu.

3.  Change the Geometry type to Instance.

4.  Then, the Scale should be -1(x), 1(y), and 1(z).

5.  Select Duplicate Special.

# Grouping the Asset

Finally, you have your full mech again. Now you need to make sure the mech stays contained and together in the scene. To do this, you can group all of its parts and name the group.

1.  In the Outliner, select all the mech's parts. Then, press Ctrl+G (to group together).

2.  Double-click the newly made group and name it char_mech_01 (see Figure 4-16).

***Figure 4-16.*** *A grouped object node for the mech's meshes*

# Summary

This chapter concentrated on looking ahead and preparing for the next phases of the pipeline. You worked through setting up and optimizing the meshes for UV unwrapping, high poly modeling, rigging, and animation. To accomplish this, you learned about the pipeline's best practices, using the Outliner, cleaning up the scene, naming conventions, modifying transforms, and optimizing pivot locations. With a clean and organized scene file, you can now move ahead to the next part of the pipeline—the UV unwrapping.

# CHAPTER 5

# UV Mapping

In this chapter, you continue working on the 3D mech that you started in Chapter 2, by moving to the next step in the pipeline: UV mapping. This chapter covers the foundations of arranging UVs, the UV Editor and Toolkit, and the guidelines for the next step in the pipeline. As illustrated in Figure 5-1, you had two paths you could have chosen—UV mapping of the low poly mesh or working on the high poly model (Chapter 6). As mentioned at the beginning of the book, a lot of the pipeline is nonlinear. Therefore, you can decide what you want to do next. Let's now focus on UVs.

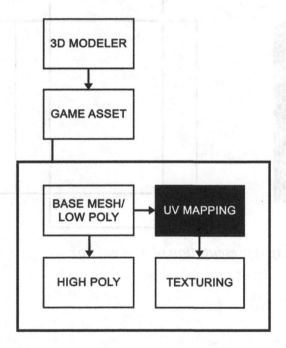

*Figure 5-1.* *A 3D modeler process flowchart with UV mapping highlighted*

117

© Nova Villanueva 2022
N. Villanueva, *Beginning 3D Game Assets Development Pipeline*,
https://doi.org/10.1007/978-1-4842-7196-4_5

# What Are UVs?

Before getting technical about what UVs are, I recommend some traditional arts and crafts. Use (or imagine) an item such as a cereal box and open it up until it is flat on a table. This flattened-out box is the two-dimensional representation of it (see Figure 5-2). Each of the edges has two corners, which resemble vertices (see Figure 5-3), and this is where UVs store their coordinates. These are called *UV points*. UV points can connect to make larger forms, which are called *UV shells*.

By using UVs in this way, you can apply a texture (an image) to a mesh. The UVs provide the placement between the surface of the mesh and how the image is wrapped (or mapped) onto it. UVs are two-dimensional texture coordinates, much like how X, Y, and Z are three-dimensional coordinates. U and V represent the axes in 2D. Therefore, this flattened-out cereal box shows the 2D view of a 3D mesh.

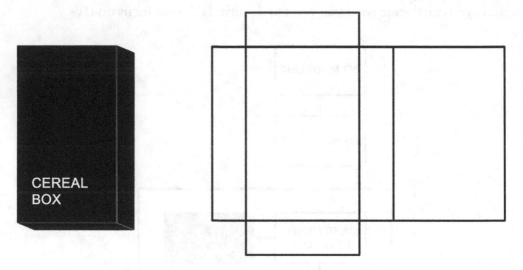

*Figure 5-2.* *A UV map representation of a cereal box*

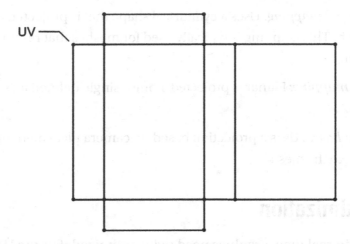

UV

**Figure 5-3.** *UV coordinate placement representation in 2D space*

By default, Maya will create UVs for most meshes that include primitive shapes such as cubes. The program will create default UVs when a cube is first created. However, as you alter and modify meshes, the UVs will not be retained as you would hope, and you'll have to lay them out properly.

Since Maya will not update the UVs as you are modeling, it is common practice to finish modeling a mesh before moving onto arranging UVs. This arrangement in a two-dimensional representation is called *UV mapping.*

As you keep reading this chapter, you will see that it is a lot easier to UV unwrap a model with a lower poly count and well-created topology. It is rare for anyone to map out UVs using a high poly model since it would be less efficient. After you create your first UV maps, it should become clear why the asset pipeline typically happens in this order—low poly modeling, UVs, and high poly modeling (detailing).

## The Different Ways You Can UV Map

The process of mapping the mech is a combination of the simplest and best-results methods. I cover the foundations of UV mapping; however, there are various ways to map out a mesh. For a more advanced understanding of UV mapping, this is what a 3D modeler has as their objective: balancing optimization and minimizing stretching or pinching. This chapter mainly covers automatic mapping. However, there are different mapping methods that include:

- *Automatic mapping*: The standard mapping for getting initial UVs. It autonomously creates a UV map by projecting from multiple planes.

- *Cylindrical mapping:* Uses a cylindrical shape that is projected onto the mesh. This mapping is typically used for meshes that resemble a cylinder.

- *Planar mapping:* Planar is projected along a single defined axis: X, Y, or Z.

- *Camera based:* Uses a projection based on camera placement in relation to the mesh.

## UV Map Optimization

Since games are in real time, graphics need to be optimized. For the UV map, this means that the more shells there are, the more data the game engine needs to process. Optimizing a UV map consists of spacing, as few shells as possible, and texture resolution. Figure 5-4 shows non-optimized UVs on the left and optimized UVs on the right.

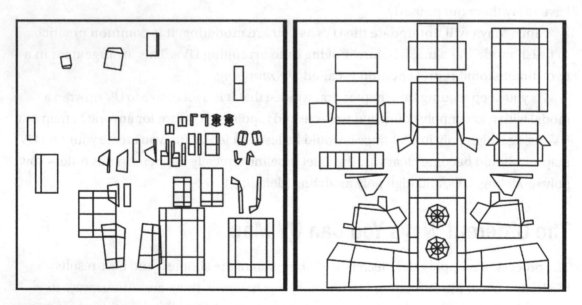

***Figure 5-4.*** *Optimization comparison*

Mobile and web games typically have very heavily optimized UV maps, but even large AAA games that have a larger poly count within their models follow this process. This becomes a concern when texture maps must be loaded into the graphic's memory card.

## What Is the UV Editor?

The UV Editor allows you to view and interact with your meshes' UVs (UV texture coordinates) within a 2D space. Much like the 3D View Panel you have been using to select, transform, and edit your 3D meshes, you can use the UV Editor to select, transform (move, rotate, scale), and modify their UV topology. Also, just like the grid in 3D space, a mesh's UV topology is being displayed on a 2D grid, where the X, Y, and Z axes translate to a 2D axis: X is U, Y is V, and Z is not relevant.

You can view a texture image as a background within the UV Editor to align your UV layout, which will be useful during later steps in the process. The texture image stays within the confines of the first quadrant (0, 1) of the UV space, also known as 0-to-1 space. Therefore, UVs must also be laid out or packed within these boundaries.

You can select UVs in the UV Editing workspace to compare the UVs and the 3D mesh and see how they translate; see Figure 5-5.

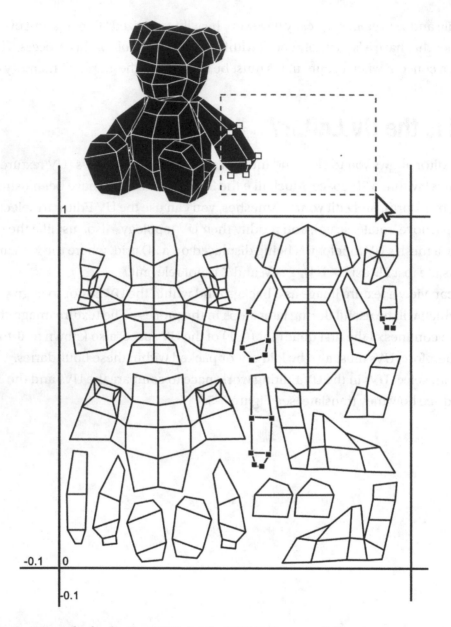

**Figure 5-5.** *Visual of selecting UVs in the UV Editor and 3D view*

The UV Toolkit is a handy tool to use in conjunction with the UV Editor; it allows you to modify and organize UVs.

# Clean Up for UV Mapping

For the following steps, you can continue with the model you made in Chapter 4 or open the start file named start_ch5.

Before you get started UV mapping, note that the faces of the mech that you do not see no longer have to be a part of the model. Ultimately, having extra faces that will be unseen in the game is unnecessary. You can delete the unseen faces. See Figure 5-6.

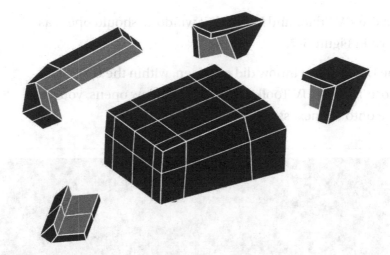

***Figure 5-6.*** *Head model with additional underside geometry selected*

Follow these steps for each of the four pieces of the head:

1. In the View Panel, right-click the head and go to Face Mode.

2. Since this is a combined mesh, to select one of the head pieces, double-click one of them. Then, within this panel's top menu, click the Isolated Select icon ![icon].

3. On the head piece, making sure you are still in Face Mode, select the inner faces, as shown in Figure 5-6, and press Delete.

4. Again, select Isolated Select ![icon] to disable it.

5. Repeat Steps 1-3 for the rest of the head pieces.

The mesh pieces should now be without inner faces. You can move onto seeing the models in the UV Editor.

# Setting Up and Using the UV Editor

You can begin by opening the tools you need to edit UVs, the UV Editor window.

1. First, make sure you are in the Modeling menu or press F2 to get to it.

2. In the top menu, choose UV ➤ UV Editor (or Windows ➤ Modeling Editors ➤ UV Editor).

   Both the UV Editor and UV Toolkit windows should open, as shown in Figure 5-7.

3. If the UV Toolkit window did not open, within the UV Editor, choose Tools ➤ UV Toolkit. Once the window opens, you can move onto the next step.

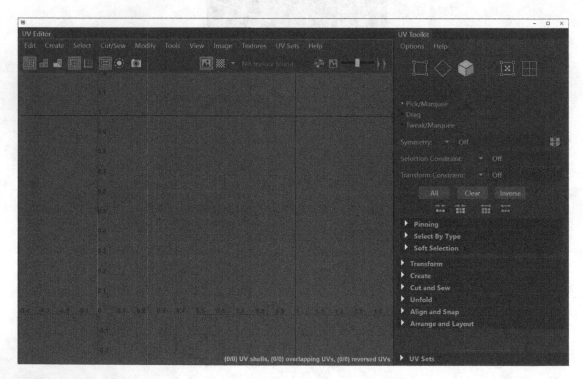

***Figure 5-7.*** *UV Editor*

To see the UVs of any given mesh in the editor, the mesh needs to be selected first. You will explore this in the next steps.

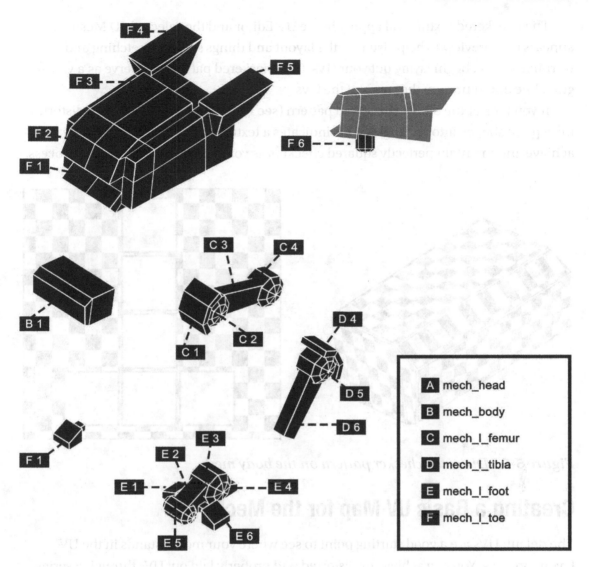

**Figure 5-8.** *Diagram of the mech's pieces*

1. In the View Panel, choose the body (B1), as shown in Figure 5-8.

2. With the body selected, the UV Editor will show Maya's default
   UVs for primitive polygon shapes (see Figure 5-9).

3. In the UV Editor, select the checker map icon ▦ in the top-middle
   portion of this window.

The checkered texture will appear in the UV Editor and the selected 3D Mesh appears as a preview to help visualize the layout and things such as stretching and warping. As you begin laying out your UVs, this checkered pattern will serve as a visual guideline and represent the status of the UVs.

If you look at the body's checkered pattern (see Figure 5-9), some areas are distorting the square shapes into rectangles. This indicates a texture that is distorted. The idea is to achieve and maintain perfectly squared checkers as you continue the UV layout process.

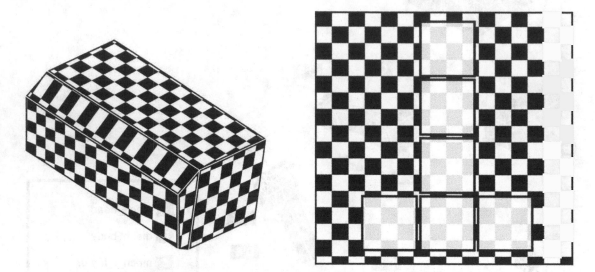

***Figure 5-9.***  *Distorted checker pattern on the body mesh*

## Creating a Basic UV Map for the Mech

The default UVs are a good starting point to see where your model stands in the UV layout process. You can achieve undistorted and properly laid out UVs through a series of UV projection mappings or unfolding actions. As mentioned, the main one utilized for this mech is automatic mapping.

With the body still selected, in the UV Editor top menu, choose Create ➤ Automatic.

## Automatic Mapping

During the process of automatic mapping, Maya calculates the surface of a mesh using a combination of plane projections to best lay out the mesh's UVs in a 2D space (see Figure 5-10). The shapes that it outputs are called *shells*. Automatic mapping means you don't have to manually lay out each polygon side. As a result, it gives you a faster start. It is like adding the big brush strokes for you, which you then go back and add detail to later.

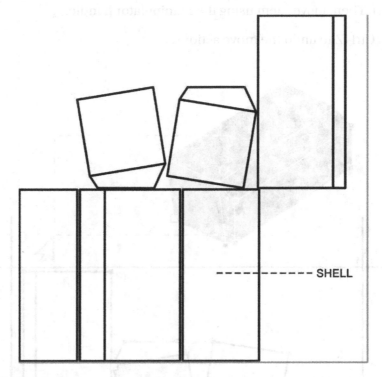

***Figure 5-10.*** *Automatic mapping of a body*

## Interacting with UV Components in the UV Editor

Now that you have some correctly projected UVs, you can use the following steps to interact with them:

1.  In the View Panel, select the body (B1). You will see the automatic mapped UVs laid out, as shown in Figure 5-10.

2.  Go into UV Mode (right-click any shell and select UV from the marking menu). Marquee select the UVs (by dragging), as shown in Figure 5-11.

3.  In the UV Editor, you can see the corresponding selected UVs highlighted in the 2D space (see Figure 5-11).

The UV selection will highlight and visualize similar to vertices; however, UVs cannot be moved in 3D space, only within the UV Editor. To move the UVs, follow these steps:

1. In the UV Editor, with the UVs still selected, press M (to move them). Then, move them using the manipulator handle.

2. Press Ctrl+Z to undo the move actions.

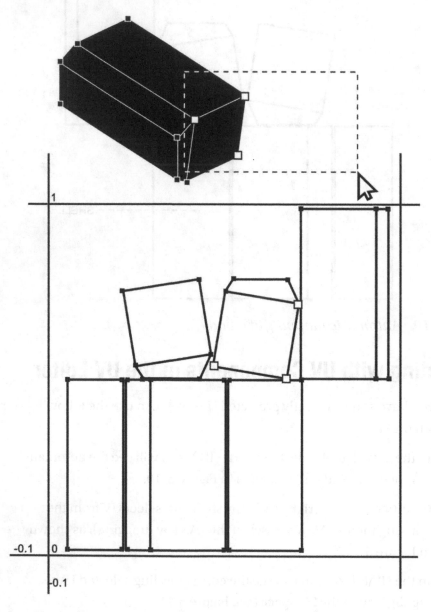

***Figure 5-11.*** *Marquee selection of UVs within the UV Editor*

128

# UVing Multiple Meshes Simultaneously

As you continue laying out your UVs, the chapter will cover various UV unwrap methods that are the best approach for the current mesh. For now, let's continue with the rest of the mech. To speed up the workflow, follow these steps for all the meshes:

1.  In the View Panel, drag-select all the meshes. Again in the UV Editor top menu, choose Create ➤ Automatic.

If you select any of the meshes, the UV Editor should show their automatic mappings that you created in the previous step.

---

**Tip**    You can also access automatic mapping via the Create tab in the UV Toolkit.

---

# Deleting History of the UVed Meshes

Throughout these steps, you should regularly delete the history of your meshes to keep them optimized. As you might remember from Chapter 4, deleting the history after every few actions is a common practice in 3D modeling in Maya. To do it, choose Edit ➤ Delete by Type ➤ History in the top menu.

# Optimizing the Mesh UVs

Although this could be sufficient for texturing the mech, there are a few things you need to consider. Too many shells slow down the game engine and the texturing process will benefit from more organized and deliberately laid out UVs.

Do you remember the cereal box and how easy it was to identify the front of the box compared to the top and sides? Likewise, if the cereal box is taken into another program to get textured, it is easy to add a graphic logo to the correct side or UV shell.

Let's try to achieve such a layout with the mech's UVs. Right now, you have too many shells and can't tell what shape corresponds to what part of the mech. Having too many shells can be resolved by sewing shells together at the seams.

# Cutting and Sewing Seams

Seams occur when bordering edges of a model are separated along UV edges due to them being a part of different UV shells. Like in real-life garment sewing, sewing seams is the process of stitching shells together along their border edges in order for them to become one larger, seamless shell. In this example, UV shells represent the fabric.

Anywhere there is a UV seam, a visible and undesired offset could appear on the textured model (see Figure 5-12). Therefore, not only is thoughtful seam placement important for shell optimization, which is crucial for a game engine's performance, but it also plays a big role in how a texture map eventually gets displayed on a model.

***Figure 5-12.*** *A comparison showing an offset seam on the left*

Since automatic mapping by default only preserves the integrity of the shell in terms of distortion, shells may be separated that could otherwise be together. On the flipside, there could be shells that were projected together that would be better separated. Shell seams can either be sewn together or cut and separated.

You can see where all the pieces for the highlighted leg connector have been automatically laid out:

1. In the View Panel, select the mech_1_femur mesh (C). You will see the automatic mapped UVs laid out, as displayed in Figure 5-13.

2. Then, still in the View Panel, switch to Face Mode and double-click the upper leg connector's face.

3.  With the faces selected from the last step, you can see the highlighted leg connector shells in the UV Editor.

4.  You can optimize the UVs with the following steps. Let's start by sewing some seams for the left leg. Since the right leg was an instance, UV editing done to the left will show up on the right. Hence, you only need to UV the left leg.

5.  Still in the UV Editor, switch to Edge Mode. This step can be done in either the UV Editor or in the View Panel.

6.  In this mode, when you hover over the edges, they will turn a different color and indicate the corresponding edge in 3D space with the same highlighted color. Selecting edges can be done in the View Panel, UV Editor, or a combination. Continue the following steps using Figure 5-13 as a guide.

7.  For the upper left leg (mech_1_femur), hold Shift and select the edges named A, B, and C (see Figure 5-13). These are the edges for the leg connector.

    As you select an edge, its corresponding border edge will be selected and highlighted automatically.

You can connect edges in a process called *sewing* or remove their connection in a process called *cutting*. Try sewing one with the following steps:

1.  With the edges selected, in the UV Editor top menu, choose Cut/Sew ➤ Move and Sew. You should see some of the shells "jump" to the shells they have now been stitched to, as shown in Figure 5-13.

2.  Then, for the upper left leg, hold Shift and select the edges named D, E, and F (see Figure 5-13). These are the edges for the lower motor unit.

3.  With the edges selected, choose Cut/Sew ➤ Move and Sew. The shells will "jump" to the shells they have now been stitched to.

4.  Then, still in the upper left leg, hold Shift and select the edges named G, H, and I (see Figure 5-13). These are the edges for the higher motor unit.

5.  With the edges selected, choose Cut/Sew ➤ Move and Sew again.

This sewing process has to be repeated until all the shells can be connected without distorting the shape of them. As you work on sewing together these shells, some of them may start to overlap as they get moved around. This overlap is normal at this stage, as shown in Figure 5-14.

1.  Still in the upper left leg, hold Shift and select the edges named J, K, L, and M (see Figure 5-13). These are the edges for the higher motor armor.

2.  With the edges selected, choose Cut/Sew ➤ Move and Sew again.

3.  Now is a good time to delete the history of the mesh.

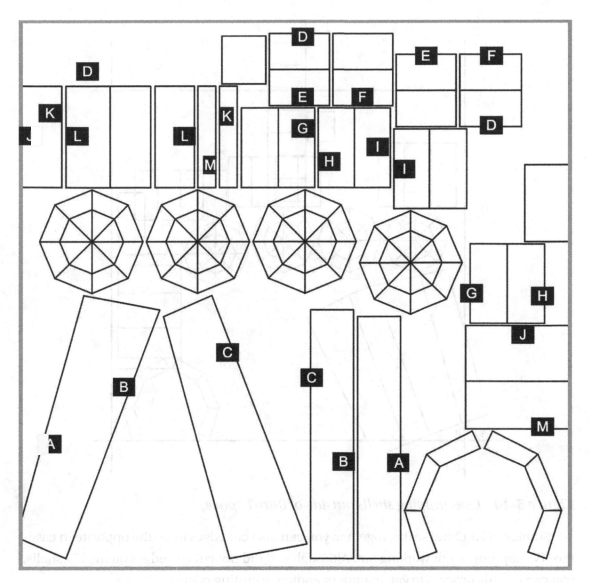

***Figure 5-13.*** *Selecting edges for moving and sewing illustrative guidelines*

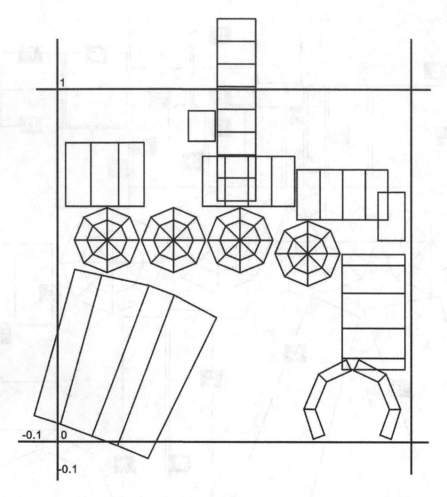

**Figure 5-14.** *Overlapping shells outside of 0-to-1 space*

Similar to stitching seams together, you can also cut edges to do the opposite in case the UV mapping is not working out. Although you did not cut any edges on the UV shells, you can try this process to get an understanding of cutting edges:

1.  In the UV Editor, switch to Edge Mode.

2.  Select an edge of a shell.

3.  With the edge selected, in the UV Editor top menu, choose Cut/ Sew ➤ Cut.

4.  With the hotbox menu open in the UV Editor, drag the mouse over the UV to switch to UV Mode.

5.   Select a UV along the cut edge.

6.   In the UV Editor, with the UV still selected, hold-drag the manipulator handle and move it around to see the now separated edge.

7.   Press Ctrl+Z to undo the cut actions.

# Unfolding UV Shells

Unfolding UV shells is the process of laying the UVs out flat as if they were on a flat surface. Since you used automatic mapping to lay out your UVs, it already does the majority of the work in terms of finding the best balance between shell seams and optimized UV layout. Therefore, you do not need to go through this step for your mesh. However, if the mesh involves sewing seams, especially with complex organic shapes such as human heads, you'll need this unwrapping technique.

To get an understanding of unfolding, follow these steps:

1.   Enter UV Mode in the UV Editor.

2.   Select some of the UVs for the upper leg connector.

3.   With the UVs selected, choose Modify ➤ Unfold. The shells could slightly shift depending on if any seam stitching distorted and warped the shells in the process.

The shells have been reflattened according to the new UV shell's layout.

Lastly, optimizing the mesh also refers to removing any unneeded geometry. These include faces that are not visible or are embedded in another mesh part. Their UV shells take up unnecessary space within UV space.

Follow these steps for the upper leg connector:

1.   In the View Panel, right-click mech_1_femur and go to Face Mode.

2.   Since this is a combined mesh, double-click the leg connector. Then, within this panel's top menu, click the Isolated Select icon ![icon].

3.   On the isolated leg connector mesh, making sure you are still in Face Mode, select the end cap faces and press Delete.

4.   Then again, select Isolated Select ![icon] to disable it.

The mesh leg connector should now be without inner faces. Next, you will continue to focus on the `mech_1_femur` (C) part for the next steps of optimizing and arranging UVs.

# Handling a Real-Life UV Pipeline Scenario

A technical artist walks into your office and says:

> *"Hello! I was talking to the rendering programmers and I noticed that you are creating a mech the same size as a dozen others in our game. And that one has textures that are over 4k, which is causing performance and streaming issues. Therefore, if you are going to approach this mech the same way, it will be too large. The textures would be over budget."*

In the meantime, the producer schedules an hour-long meeting to talk about the hundred mechs in the open-world game. The take-away as a 3D artist is that at this scale, the texture size that can support this mech would be over 4K, based on the texel density. Since this could cause issues, the Art Director has asked you to reduce the size of the mech to make it at eye level.

As discussed in earlier chapters, revisions could occur. You now need to resize the mech character:

1. In the Outliner, select `char_mech_01`. Then, in the Channel Box, change its scale to X = 0.6, Y = 0.6, and Z = 0.6.

2. With the group selected, choose Modify ➤ Freeze Transformations from the top menu.

# Optimizing and Arranging UVs

At this stage, you should have a basic UV map of `mech_1_femur`. As mentioned, overlapping can occur and is normal. To clean this up, you need to work on the UV shells' texel density and optimized layout.

## Texel Density

Texel density is often not discussed enough, despite it being a necessary concept. Texel density is an integral part of the 3D art asset pipeline.

For that reason, let's start with the basics by first defining what a texel is. A *texel*, or texture element, is the fundamental unit of texture space. Texels represent textures on 3D models, just as pixels represent textures on 2D images. With that said, texels can hold a certain amount of pixels depending on how dense a texture needs to be.

This leads to *texel density,* which is the process of setting up the overall size of a UV shell by making its texels (pixels per unit) the same across an entire map. It allows every UV shell to be proportional based on size and scale through mathematical calculations. As a result, a model's textures will look consistently crisp and clean throughout, and not inconsistently pixelated and blurry. An example of this procedure in game development is when environment artists use it to create their environment art. The way you can achieve a texel density for your model is using the UV Toolkit window.

Figure 5-15 shows an example of a UVed model with no texel density set. The image on the right has UVs with a set texel density.

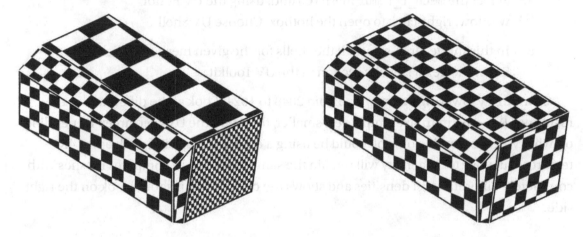

***Figure 5-15.*** *Texel density visually illustrated on the mech body (right image)*

Follow these steps to correct the texel density on mech_1_femur:

1. In the UV Toolkit window, under the Transform section (which you may have to click to open), locate the Texel Density section.

2. In Texel Density (px/unit), input 5.12 if you do not already have it (see Figure 5-16).

The scene is set up in meters; however the Texel Density tool in Maya defaults to centimeters. Therefore, you are using a texel density of 512 and converting it to centimeters, which is 5.12.

At the time of writing this book, a set texel density of 512 is the common standard across the industry. This is due to the fact that it sits fairly well between 256 and 1024, 256 being potentially too pixelated and 1024 being potentially too demanding on graphics processes.

3.  Set the Map Size to 2048 (see Figure 5-16). This is the resolution in pixels for the texture map.

*Figure 5-16.* *Texel density in the UV Toolkit*

4.  Select the mech_1_femur mesh (C) and, using the UV Editor window, right-click to open the hotbox. Choose UV Shell.

5.  In this mode, drag-select all the shells for the given mesh and click Set in the Texel Density section in the UV Toolkit.

You can try lowering the map size from 2048 to 1024. Look at the difference in the resulting UVs—the map size simply gets smaller, therefore the UVs get larger. Depending on what you are working on, you could be using a different map size, such as for 4K textures, but your texel density will remain the same. Figure 5-15 compares meshes with completely different texel densities and shows the correct way it should look on the right side.

## Moving, Arranging, and Packing UVs

Now that you have your shells set at the correct scale and texel density, you can start arranging and packing them within the UV 0-to-1 space. This is one of the last, yet most critical, steps in the UVing process, as it involves fitting and strategically placing the shells that you have unwrapped and created so far into a confined space. However, you should be aware that there are exceptions to this 0-to-1 space.

In a game development pipeline, depending on the project, certain protocols may be in place, whereby certain UV shells of a model need to be in a certain orientation or positioned a specific way on the UV space. These customized layouts could be for performance or efficiency reasons.

Think of this process as trying to fit and rearrange perfectly packed moving boxes into the back of a certain sized moving truck. It's like playing Tetris! This arrangement of UVs can get challenging if you barely have enough space, which will depend on your texel density, map size, and scale of your object.

Since this process involves strategic planning, this step often takes the most time. You may find at times that shells have been moved outside of the main 0-to-1 quadrant. This is okay; you can look at your UV space as a work table. Things may get messy until they tidy up.

For the duration of this step, you need to be in Shell Mode using the hotbox to move shells around. The process of stitching and sewing them together may cause them to end up on top of each other. Although there are exceptions, for the texturing part of the pipeline, you cannot have any shells overlapping.

Just like how having overlapping shells was not an issue earlier during the seams sewing step, having shells scattered outside of the main 0-to-1 space is acceptable during this step—as long as you eventually have all shells properly within the space at the end. Let's get started arranging the UV shells!

To select the UV shells:

1.  In the View Panel, in Object Mode, select the mech_1_femur (C).

2.  In the UV Editor with the UVs displayed, select an entire shell:

    a.  Switch to UV Shell Mode. A preview selection will highlight a shell when it is hovered over.

    b.  Click the UV shell to select it.

    c.  Or you can go to UV Mode and double-click one of the UVs of a shell to select the entire shell.

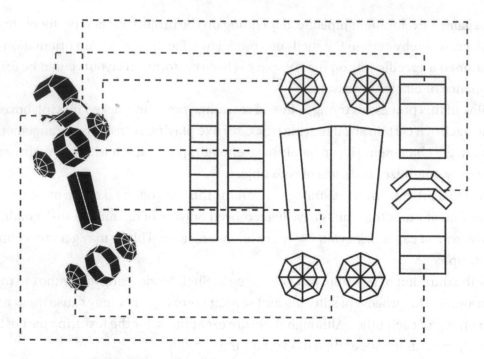

***Figure 5-17.*** *UV shells laid out and arranged*

Use Figure 5-17 as a guide for moving the shells. You can move the shells to the 0-to-1 space (see Figure 5-18) by doing the following:

1.  Switch to Move Mode (M). In the UV Editor, with the UVs still selected, hold-drag the manipulator handle to move it around.

2.  Or in the UV Toolkit (inside the UV Editor), choose ➤ Transform section ➤ Move. In the Move section, you can insert an incremental unit to move your UV shells by and then use the arrows to the right to move them at the amount of the specified increments.

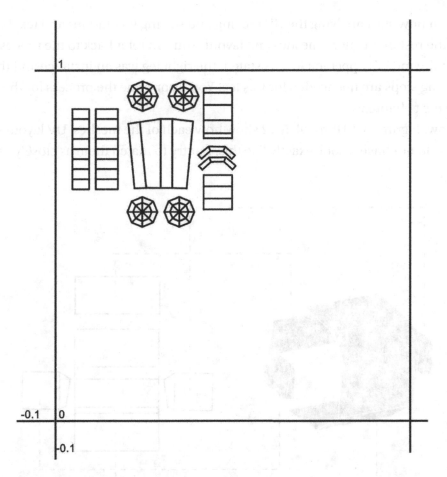

**Figure 5-18.** *Mech's femur layout and arranged UVs within 0-to-1 space*

You can rotate the shells by doing the following:

1.  Go to Rotate Mode (E). In the UV Editor with the UVs still selected, hold-drag the manipulator circle to rotate it around.

2.  Or in the UV Toolkit (inside the UV Editor), choose ➤ Transform section ➤ Rotate. In the Rotate section, you can insert an incremental degree value to rotate your UV shells by and use the rotation buttons to rotate them clockwise or counterclockwise by the amount of the specified increments, such as 45 or 90 degrees.

You can now start applying the UV moving and sewing techniques and texel density steps for the rest of the mech meshes and layout. You can refer back to the process shown for the mech's upper left leg. As stated, the right leg was an instance and therefore the following steps are not needed for this leg. You'll continue the process for the right leg in the next chapter.

For now, Figures 5-19 through 5-22 show how each of the meshes' UV layout should look. They do not have to look exactly like this, but try to match them as closely as possible.

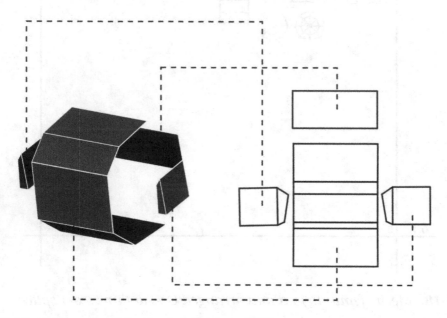

***Figure 5-19.*** *Diagram of the body's laid out UV map*

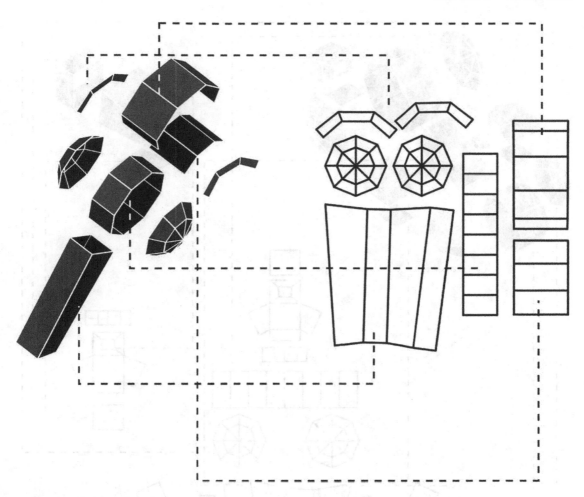

**Figure 5-20.** *Diagram of the body's laid out UV map*

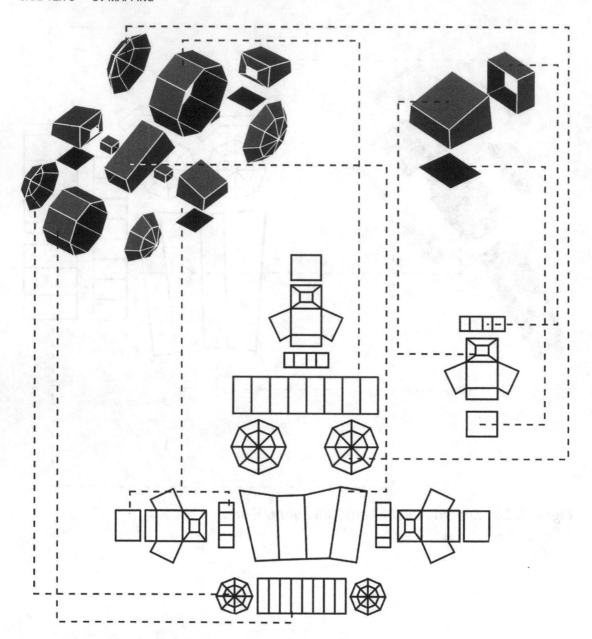

***Figure 5-21.*** *Diagram of the foot's laid out UV map*

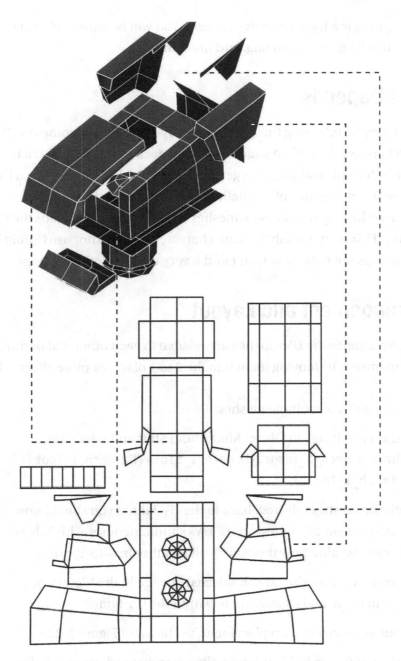

**Figure 5-22.** *Diagram of the head's laid out UV map*

Continuously arrange your shells. Remember, it does not matter if all the shells fit into the 0-to-1 space during this process of UV unwrapping. It's just important that they all could eventually fit in the space, without going over the grid lines in the final layout.

UV unwrapping is a highly iterative process. You will bounce back and forth between seam sewing, texel density, arranging, and unfolding.

# It Always Depends

Although you may be following this process step by step, when it comes to UV mapping, the results will always depend on your mesh. The mech in this book has a hard surface and therefore automatic mapping can get you to your goal. However, when it comes to meshes that are more organic, other methods need to be used.

The tool used heavily with organic meshes is Unfold, which spreads the UVs out around a seam. This is commonly used on characters. You do not use Unfold in this book, but that does not mean you won't find it very useful in other settings.

# Final Arrangement and Layout

Finally, you can arrange the UVs so they are relative to each other and optimized. This can be done manually by moving them into the 0 to 1 place, or more effectively by using layout tools.

To move the shells of multiple meshes:

1.  In the View Panel, in Object Mode, hold Shift and select the following: mech_l_femur (C), mech_l_tibia (D), mech_l_foot (E), and mech_l_toe (F).

2.  With the meshes selected, back in the UV Editor, you should now be able to view all of these parts' UVs simultaneously. This is how you can visualize how they will fit all together in 0-to-1 space.

    As long as the meshes are all selected at once in the View Panel, you can move and arrange them within the UV Editor.

3.  Arrange them based on placement, as shown in Figure 5-23.

4.  In the UV Editor, hold and right-click anywhere where the shells are. A hotbox menu opens. Then, with the hotbox menu open, drag the mouse over the UV Shell (mode).

5.  Press W (to move) and/or E (to rotate) on the mech's UV shells, as shown in Figure 5-23.

6.  Repeat the steps on moving multiple shells for mech_head (A) and mech_body (B), using Figure 5-24 this time.

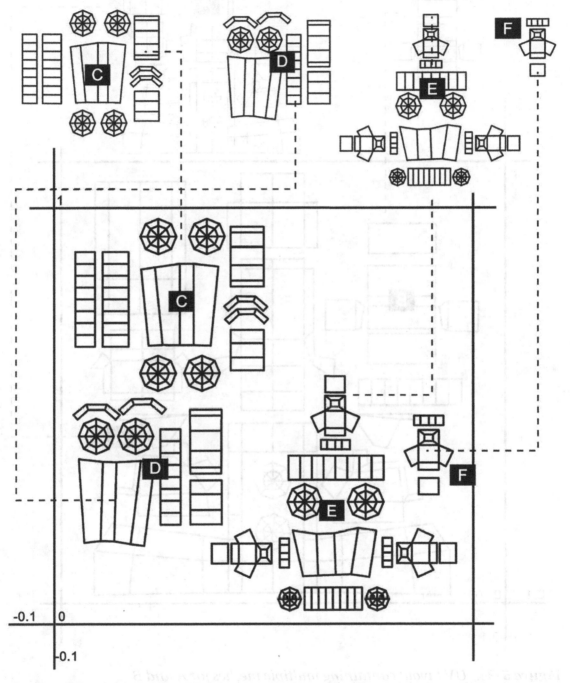

***Figure 5-23.*** *UV layout containing multiple meshes for D-F*

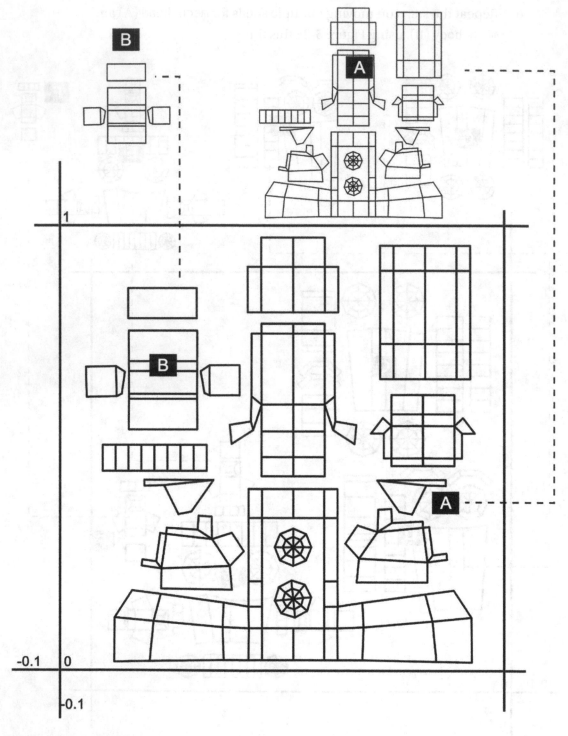

***Figure 5-24.*** *UV layout containing multiple meshes for A and B*

# Summary

In this chapter, you created a UV map for the low poly model of the mech. You learned about UVs and their importance in the texturing pipeline phase. You started by creating an automatic UV map, sewing together UV shells, setting a texel density, and arranging the objects. Then, you learned what UV maps should look like and their purpose. Finally, the chapter ended with a texture-ready UV map for texturing.

# CHAPTER 6

# Creating a High Poly Model

The goal of this chapter is to create a high poly model—in other words, to add details to your mech. This will be a separate model from the low poly. To achieve this, you will use the modeling skills you learned in Chapters 2 and 3. The chapter covers high poly modeling, using smooth preview display modes, setting up for the high poly, adding details to holding edges, and modeling in a non-destructive way.

Because the mech is hard surface, you will continue to use Maya and take the 3D modeling approach to create the high poly (see Figure 6-1). You will use modeling tools such as the Multi-Cut and Extrude tools. Then you will end up having the two models: low and high poly. They will be used in the next chapter to create what is known as a normal map. At this stage, you need to understand how to properly prepare your models for the process.

© Nova Villanueva 2022
N. Villanueva, *Beginning 3D Game Assets Development Pipeline*,
https://doi.org/10.1007/978-1-4842-7196-4_6

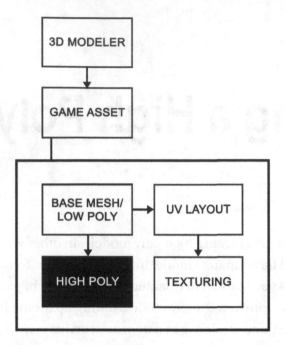

***Figure 6-1.*** *A 3D modeler process flowchart with high poly highlighted*

# What Is a High Poly Model?

A high poly model has the big reads contained in the low poly model as well as medium and small sized reads. It is utilized to project high-resolution details down to a low poly mesh. This process is otherwise known as *normal map baking*. With the high poly, you will be adding details to the model by 3D modeling in the same way you created the low poly or, alternatively, by a sculpting process. Programs such as ZBrush and Mudbox are mainly used for sculpting, unlike Maya.

# Why Create the Illusion of Depth in Games?

In terms of real-time graphics and video games, the high poly detail can be turned into a texture. This texture is then applied to the in-game model, which creates the illusion of depth when it is lit. This particular texture is our normal map. Therefore, instead of using a model with a high poly count in-game, you can simply fake the details. This workflow requires you to bake the high poly to the low poly. You need to keep these things in mind when you bake the model. This brief explanation will be further explained later in this book.

# The Different Approaches to End Up with a Low and High Poly

Beyond the high poly 3D modeling technique (see Figure 6-2) you use in this chapter, 3D sculpting is a common method. 3D sculpting is like real life fine arts sculpting with clay; you can move, add, or remove clay and shape the model with great detail. This process is great for organic models, due to their nature.

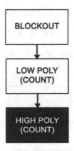

*Figure 6-2.*  *3D modeling pipeline*

Sculpting allows the artist to focus more on laying down the correct forms and less on maintaining proper edge flow throughout the creation process. This method usually produces a very dense mesh to support the high-resolution sculpted detail. Therefore, this workflow will eventually rely on the process of retopology. See Figure 6-3.

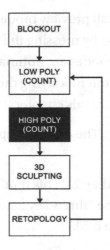

*Figure 6-3.*  *3D modeling and sculpting pipeline*

*Retopology* is the process of recreating or readjusting the edge flow of a non-optimized high-resolution model to act as a low poly mesh, which is better suitable for rendering in a game engine. Since it does not matter which approach is taken, you could have started with a high-res model. However, you need to end up with a low- and high-res model.

In 3D modeling, you are editing faces, edges, and vertices as opposed to sculpting. Whereas in sculpting, the process includes adapting the form. Both modeling and sculpting are done at a meticulous level.

In this book, we take one approach to 3D modeling an asset (see Figure 6-2), but different workflows exist, as shown in Figure 6-4. A lot of the differences in approach are based on creating hard surface or organic models.

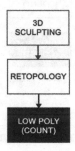

**Figure 6-4.** *3D sculpting pipeline*

# Using Smooth Mesh Preview Display Modes

There are three different Smooth Mesh preview modes that you can cycle through on a selected object, which you can access by pressing the 1, 2, and 3 keys on your keyboard. See Figures 6-5, 6-6, and 6-7. These modes are optimal for tweaking the mesh and seeing how the smooth mesh will look without modifying the original. You will utilize them while working on your mech model for this chapter:

- **Original Mesh (Hotkey 1)**: The default display mode of the original mesh (see Figure 6-5).

- **Cage+Smooth Mesh (Hotkey 2)**: This mode displays a combination of the original mesh and the "three-key smoothing" preview mode simultaneously (see Figure 6-6).

- **Smooth Mesh (Hotkey 3)**: Display mode, also known as "three-key smoothing," which lets you preview subdivisions of the selected geometry before running the actual smooth mesh operation (see Figure 6-7).

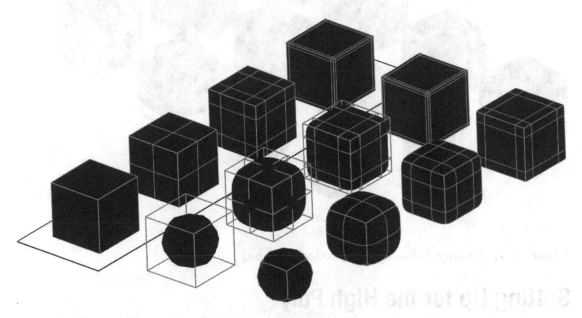

***Figure 6-5.*** *Hotkey 1 displayed for selected cubes*

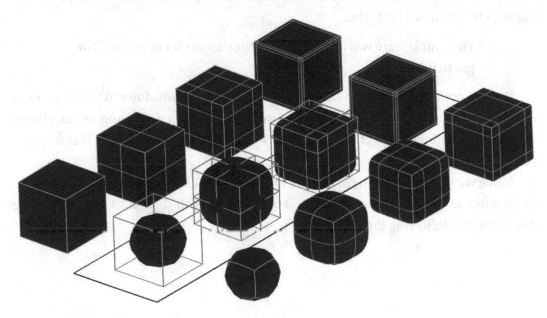

***Figure 6-6.*** *Hotkey 2 displayed for selected cubes*

155

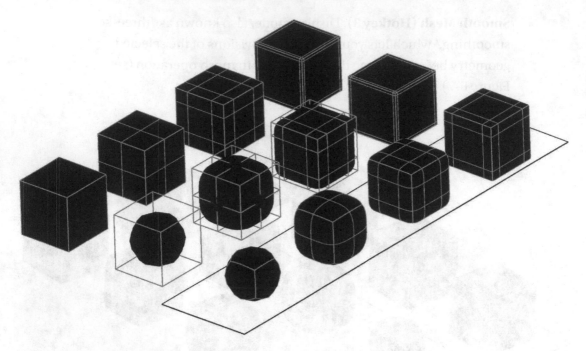

**Figure 6-7.** *Hotkey 3 displayed for selected cubes*

# Setting Up for the High Poly

For the following steps, you can continue from the model you made in Chapter 5 or open the start file named start_ch6.

1.   First, make sure you are in the Modeling menu set or press F2 to
     get to it.

We will continue to use the Outliner and Channel Box windows in this chapter. If you find that you need to reopen either of them at any point, in the top menu, choose Window ➤ Outliner. Then choose Window ➤ General Editors ➤ Channel Box/Layer Editor.

Since we instanced the right leg, the instanced right leg parts should all have the same name as the left, with a suffix of 1. For example, mech_l_femur1. You can change this simply by following these steps:

2. Using the Outliner, double-click the instance right leg part object nodes and rename them as follows:

   a. mech_l_femur1 to mech_r_femur

   b. mech_l_tibia1 to mech_r_tibia

   c. mech_l_foot1 to mech_r_foot

   d. mech_l_toe1 to mech_r_toe

3. Select metric and press Ctrl+H (to hide it).

You can now duplicate the low poly model to create a second one that gets all the additional details. To achieve this:

4. With char_mech_01 selected in the Outliner, press Ctrl+D. A duplicated group will be created, as shown in Figure 6-8.

*Figure 6-8.* *Duplicated group*

5. Rename the created char_mech_01_low to char_mech_01_high, as shown in Figure 6-9.

***Figure 6-9.***  *Renamed group to char_mech_01_high*

6.  With char_mech_01 selected in the Outliner, rename the created char_mech_01 to char_mech_01_low, as shown in Figure 6-10.

7.  To hide the low poly, select char_mech_01_low again and press Ctrl+H (see Figure 6-10).

***Figure 6-10.***  *Hidden char_mech_01_low group*

# What Is the Difference Between a Low and High Poly Model?

How do you know which details are added to each geometry? When you first begin 3D modeling, it is unclear how much detail your low poly model should have. You also need to know where the low poly ends and the high poly starts. This is usually better learned through experience and practice; however, you can also use Table 6-1 as a guide.

***Table 6-1.*** *Low and High Poly Comparison*

| Low Poly | High Poly |
| --- | --- |
| It could serve as the in-game model; therefore, it is limited by the frame rate of the game engine or the art direction. | It could be as detailed as you want it to be. It is only limited by the RAM constraints of your computer. |
| Rough edges, commonly referred to as sharp edges. | Smooth (edges) containing holding edges. Better edge definition. |
| Usually does not contain small details and mainly consists of overall medium to big shapes and reads that affect the silhouette. | Can consist of smaller reads and contain small details such as holes, screws, bolts, dents, and imperfections. |

With Table 6-1, you can begin to understand the poly count difference. To make things more complex, different game studios will state different poly counts for each prop, character, or environment, due to their respective production budget, visual aesthetics, and game types they are developing, such as FPS, third-person, isotropic, and side-scroller. This makes it hard for someone starting out to get a proper poly count, as there are many variables involved, such as how far the model is from the camera or whether the game has a cartoony or realistic look. To give you a better understanding of how your models need to look, let's take a visual approach.

One concern about not having the proper poly count for each model is that poly count rules can vary tremendously. Thus, consider these rules of thumb:

- Details that you cannot show on your low poly because it will be too dense to model go on your high poly.

- Details that do not affect the silhouette of your low poly also go on your high poly.

If the detail affects your silhouette, it must be modeled into your low poly model.

# Creating the High Poly Model

First, the high poly mesh should have the same big reads as the low poly mesh. The silhouette of your low poly model and high poly model cannot differ much. If they do, you need to alter one of them. Second, you need to keep both models in the same position, directly overlapping each other.

Now that you know the objective, it is common to get to the next step in the pipeline—texturing. This is one of the parts of the pipeline that is nonlinear, and you may realize afterward that your models need further alterations. Therefore, you should be able to go back and forth with iterations until you get it right. Use Figure 6-11 as a guide for the rest of the steps in this chapter.

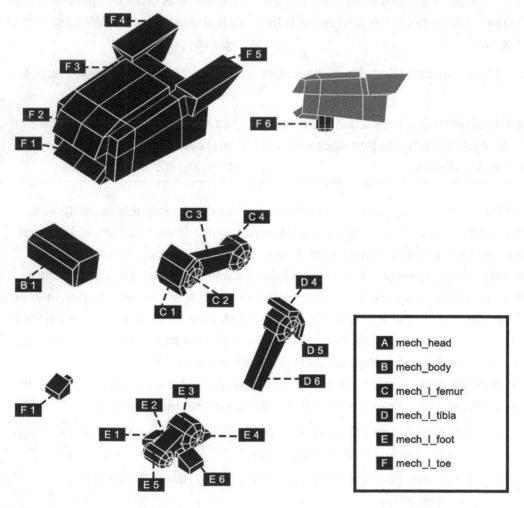

*Figure 6-11.* *Body meshes*

# Adding Details and Edge Definition to the Body

For the body mesh (B), you will use the Multi-Cut tool the same way you did in Chapter 3. However, this time you will be adding holding edges. *Holding edges* are edge loops that are added to shapes to gain more control over the bevel or transition from one surface to the next. This could be during the process of smoothing out a mesh. Basically, you want to be able to either round the edges out or maintain their definition. The closer multiple edges are to one another, the tighter the edge transition and highlights they produce. It is common for people to use a bevel edge approach to get a similar result; however, it is better to edit the edges in a non-destructive way. You will learn more about this later in the chapter.

To make it easier to see if your Wireframe on Shaded is not shown:

1.    In the View Panel toolbar, choose Shading ➤ Wireframe on Shaded. You can also press Alt(Option)+5 to show it in the model, as shown in Figure 6-12.

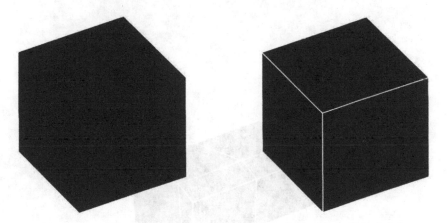

*Figure 6-12.  Model in shaded mode on left and with wireframe-on-shaded enabled on the right*

Before you start adding more geometry, you could add an edge loop to the body to be the centerline. The following steps demonstrate using the Multi-Cut tool technique to add an edge loop that runs down the center of the body mesh (B), as shown in the bottom image of Figure 6-13.

2.  Select the mech_body mesh (B) and, in the top menu, choose Mesh
    Tools ➤ Multi-Cut.

3.  With the Multi-Cut tool selected, press and hold Ctrl+Shift, which
    will now snap the preview edge loops as you move across the
    surface.

4.  Insert one edge loop in the location illustrated on the bottom
    image of Figure 6-13. This will be the model's centerline.

***Figure 6-13.*** *Body with centerline added*

5.  Press 3 on the keyboard to preview the mesh as smooth.

Currently, since you do not have any holding edges on the mesh, the forms will collapse.

6.  Then press 1 to revert to the original mesh view (see Figure 6-5).

By default, any edits you make to your mesh will affect only one side. Recall that you used symmetry mode to edit the top and bottom of the sphere simultaneously in Chapter 3. You can also use symmetry for the left and right sides of the body mesh as follows:

1.  Navigate to the Status Line and choose Symmetry from the dropdown menu, which should be set to Off by default.

2.  Select World X (to show it highlighted in blue when enabled).

Now, any changes you make to one side of the body will reflect to the other side. For example, when you insert and snap edge loops on the left and right sides, they will be equidistant from either side. In the following steps, you will add holding edges to shape the body:

3.  Select the mech_body (B).

4.  Then, go back to the Multi-Cut tool (choose Mesh Tools ➤ Multi-Cut).

5.  With the Multi-Cut tool selected, press and hold Ctrl (without using Shift to snap this time) to preview the edge loops as you move across the surface.

6.  Add holding edges along the X axis, as illustrated in the top image of Figure 6-14.

7.  Next, add holding edges along the Y axis, as illustrated in the bottom image of Figure 6-14.

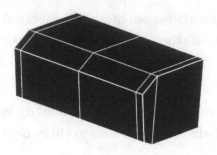

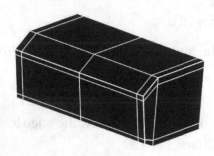

***Figure 6-14.*** *Body showing added edge loops*

It is common practice to go back and forth from viewing the cage view to the actual poly look as you detail the model. As you add more edge loops to the model, go back and forth by pressing 1 and 2. You can also go into the preview of 3, but it is not recommended. You need to make sure you are applying the edges when in the original mesh preview (1). Advanced and experienced 3d modelers can work directly on the three-key-smoothing (3) without messing up, but even they would not recommend it to beginners.

8.  Select the body mesh again.

9.  Go back to the Multi-Cut tool (choose Mesh Tools ➤ Multi-Cut). Add holding edges along the Z axis, as illustrated in the top image of Figure 6-15.

Lastly, you have the mesh with proper holding edges. You have been looking between the three smooth preview modes to see the shape and holding edges maintained. You can finally run the Smooth command, which will subdivide the mesh. To do that, follow these steps:

1. Select mech_body (B).

2. Choose, from the top menu, choose Mesh ➤ Smooth, as shown in the bottom image of Figure 6-15.

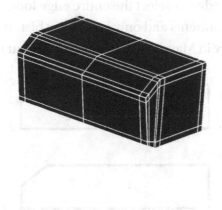

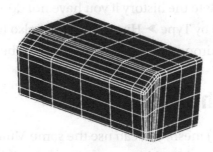

*Figure 6-15.* *Body with added edge loops*

## Modeling in a Non-Destructive Way

Working *non-destructively* refers to methods that allow you to modify or work on your model without permanently altering it to the point that you cannot go back. When adding details to the body, you went back and forth between unsmooth and smooth preview modes. This was a way of working non-destructively. However, once you actually ran the smooth operation on the mesh, you could not go back in a non-destructive way.

Another destructive approach commonly used by beginners is to bevel a mesh's edge. Bevels add a transitional edge between sharp edges that, in turn, could make the edges appear to have a soft appearance. However, unlike the holding edges method, the bevel method is not easily editable afterward.

To bevel a mesh, you select its edges and press Ctrl+B. Figure 6-16 shows a beveled edge profile. Notice that triangles are introduced at the corners and they do not make it possible to double-click an edge or select the entire edge loop. Bevels can be edited, but not without additional adjustments and only before the history is deleted. You need to constantly delete the history in Maya to keep working without running out of memory.

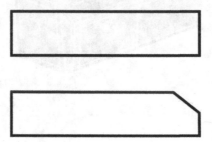

***Figure 6-16.*** *Profile of a bevel edge process*

This is a good time to delete the history if you have not done so already. In the top menu, choose Edit ➤ Delete by Type ➤ History. You can also turn off Symmetry for now. Choose Symmetry from the dropdown menu, which should be set to Off.

## Adding Details to the Feet

Next, for the mech_1_foot (E) mesh, you can use the same Multi-Cut technique you used for the body. You also need to add holding edges. Since the right foot is an instance, any geometry you add to the left foot will be added to the right.

1.  Select the mech_1_foot mesh and right-click it to switch to Face Mode.

2.  Double-click and select the leg connector of the foot.

3.  In the View Panel's top menu, click the Isolated Select icon ![icon] to isolate the mesh, as shown in Figure 6-17.

***Figure 6-17.*** *Foot mesh and isolated mesh*

4.  Go back to the Multi-Cut tool (choose Mesh Tools ➤ Multi-Cut). Press and hold Ctrl+Shift, which will now snap the preview edge loops as you move across the surface.

5.  Add a centerline to the foot's isolated leg connector mesh, as you did with the body. Do not forget to add a centerline to the underside of the mesh as well.

6.  With the Multi-Cut tool still selected, press and hold Ctrl+Shift, which will now snap to preview edge loops as you move across the surface (allowing you to move in increments of 10%).

7.  Add holding edges along the X axis, as shown in the bottom image of Figure 6-18.

---

**Tip**   During the process of adding edge loops, you can better observe the edge definition by toggling off the Wireframe on Shaded (press Alt+5).

---

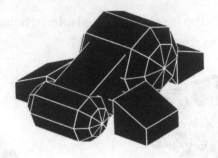

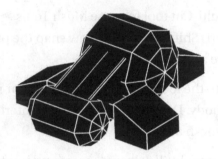

**Figure 6-18.**  *Foot mesh with centerline and holding edges added*

8.  Add holding edges along the Y axis on the leg connector, as illustrated in the top image of Figure 6-19.

9.  Choose Isolated Select  to turn off isolation mode on the leg connector mesh.

10. Add a centerline and holding edges to the motor units, as shown in the bottom image of Figure 6-19.

***Figure 6-19.***  *Motor units with centerline and holding edges added*

11.  Adjust the holding edges along the X axis of the motor units, as shown in the top image of Figure 6-20. Select edge loops on either side of the centerline and scale outward in the X axis.

12.  Add holding edges on the foot stabilizers, as illustrated in the bottom image of Figure 6-20.

**Figure 6-20.** *Foot stabilizer meshes with holding edges added*

Like with the body, you now have the foot (E) mesh with proper holding edges and can finally run the smooth command to subdivide the mesh.

Simply select the mech_1_foot (E). Then, in the top menu, choose Mesh ➤ Smooth, as shown in Figure 6-21. The foot and body mesh are now subdivided.

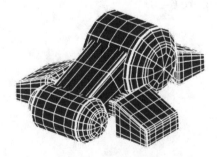

**Figure 6-21.** *Foot mesh with centerline and holding edges added*

# Adding the Rest of the Mech's Details

For the rest of the meshes (A, C, D, and F), you can repeat the techniques covered using the Multi-Cut tool in the previous steps. Check out Figures 6-22 through 6-31 for the results.

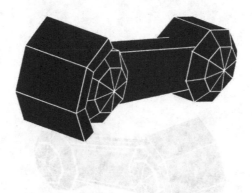

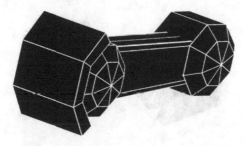

*Figure 6-22.* *Femur's leg connector mesh with holding edges added*

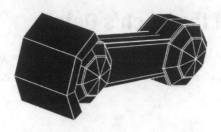

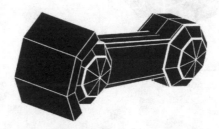

**Figure 6-23.**  *Femur's motor unit meshes with holding edges added*

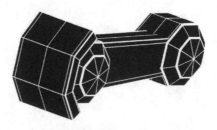

**Figure 6-24.**  *Femur's motor armor mesh with holding edges added*

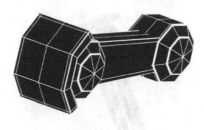

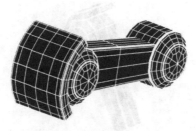

**Figure 6-25.** *Femur's motor armor mesh with holding edges added and smoothed*

**Figure 6-26.** *Tibia's leg connector mesh with holding edges added*

**Figure 6-27.**  *Tibia's motor unit mesh with holding edges added*

**Figure 6-28.**  *Tibia's mesh with holding edges added and smoothed*

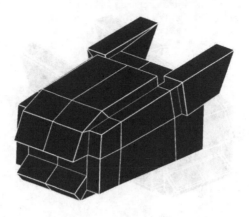

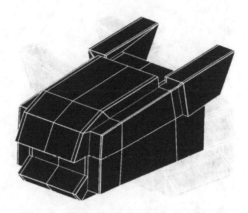

**Figure 6-29.** *The head's mesh with holding edges added*

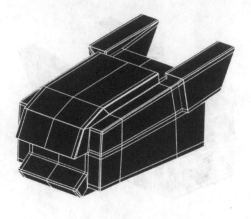

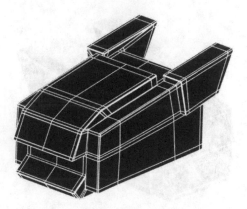

**Figure 6-30.** *The head's mesh with holding edges added*

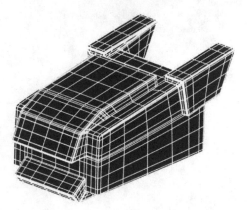

**Figure 6-31.** *The head's mesh with holding edges added and smoothed*

***Figure 6-32.*** *3D Render of the low and high poly mech*

To finish detailing the high poly mesh (see Figure 6-32), let's clean up the scene.

1.  Clear the history again. Select the mech's meshes and choose
    Edit ➤ Delete by Type ➤ History from the top menu.

2.  In the Outliner window, choose char_mech_01_low and press
    Shift+H to unhide it.

At this point, char_mech_01_low and char_mech_01_high should be overlapping
each other.

Since you are working on a hard surface high poly model in this book, this is how a
high poly organic model will look (see Figure 6-33). The sculpting approach was used
with this model.

*Figure 6-33.* *3D Render of an organic high poly example*

# Summary

This chapter showed you how to finish creating the high poly mech model from the low poly model. You learned what a high poly model is, about illusion of depth, the different approaches to end with a low and high poly, using smooth preview display modes, setting up for the high poly, adding details with holding edges, and modeling in a non-destructive way. This workflow allowed you to create a proper high poly model, which is important for the upcoming pipeline stage: texturing. Finally, the chapter ended with a completed model for use in Chapter 6, where you'll texture the mech.

# CHAPTER 7

# Texturing

In this chapter, you look at what textures are, how they are created, and how they are applied to models. To do that, you will use additional tools beyond Maya. In Chapter 5, you learned how UV maps are created from the low poly model of the mech and what they are used for. You can use these maps to apply your textures. Throughout this chapter, you will be working with multiple textures on a single model, looking at an overview of Substance 3D Painter, creating PBR textures, working with alphas, and exporting texture maps. See Figure 7-1.

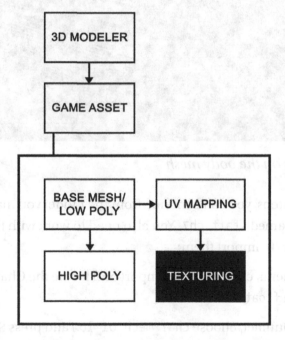

**Figure 7-1.** *A 3D modeler process flowchart with texturing highlighted*

179

© Nova Villanueva 2022
N. Villanueva, *Beginning 3D Game Assets Development Pipeline*,
https://doi.org/10.1007/978-1-4842-7196-4_7

# Using Floaters to Add Texture Details

The mech is high res enough. However, adding more detail like vents, panels, and screws would take the model to the next level, especially when it comes to texturing.

Floaters are elements of geometry that float just above the high poly model's surface. They serve as an alternative method to modeling detail directly into the high poly model. See Figure 7-2.

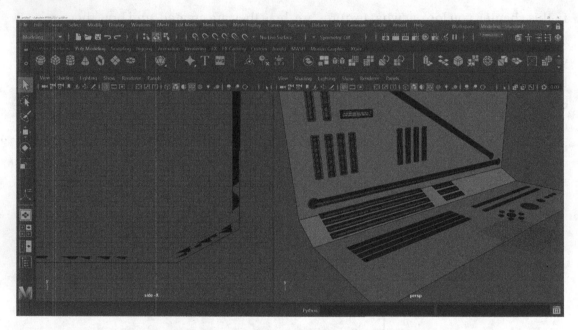

***Figure 7-2.*** *Floaters on the body mesh*

For the following steps, you can continue from the model you made in Chapter 6 or open the start file named start_ch7. You also need to work with the floater files that came with the chapter. To import them:

1.  In the top menu, choose File ➤ Import and locate the Chapter 7 files to open floaters.mb.

2.  Still in the Outliner, choose char_mech_01_low and press Shift+H (to hide it).

The floaters should be imported into the middle of the scene. They should not touch the model, but be floating close by it with a gap in the middle (see Figure 7-2). You can look at `start_ch7_floaters.mb` in the chapter files to get a better idea.

3. Use the transform tools (W, E, and R) to add the floaters as illustrated or place them in any creative way you like.

4. In the Outliner, hold Ctrl and choose the floaters group meshes that you imported in the previous steps. Then choose `char_mech_01_high` and press P (to parent it).

5. Still in the Outliner, choose `char_mech_01_high` and press Shift+H (to hide it).

6. Still in the Outliner, choose `char_mech_01_low` and press Shift+H (to unhide it).

# Getting Your Maya Files Ready

Soft edges on the mesh will help you achieve better results in the texture-baking process, as opposed to having hard edges. Artifacts due to hard edges could show up on your model during the baking process, so you need to soften them. Be aware that, in some of the following steps, it could look like nothing has happened:

1. In the Outliner, hold Shift and select all the mech's meshes under the `char_mech_01_low`.

2. With the meshes selected, choose Mesh Display ➤ Unlock Normals from the top menu.

3. Then, back to the top menu, choose Mesh Display ➤ Soften Edge from the top menu.

4. Lastly, choose Edit ➤ Delete All by Type ➤ History in the top menu.

All the meshes should have a softened appearance at the edges. You may also notice some gradient looking dark faces throughout, which is normal.

Now that you have the mech model unwrapped and have created a high poly from it, you no longer need the instanced copy of the right leg. You just need the right leg on its own and converted into a real object. To break the instance and convert it, follow these steps for the low poly mesh:

1.  In Object Mode, hold Shift and select `mech_r_femur` through `mech_r_toe`.

2.  With the meshes still selected, go to the top menu and choose Modify ➤ Convert ➤ Instance to Object.

3.  Again, hold Shift and select `mech_r_femur` through `mech_r_toe`.

4.  With the meshes still selected, choose Modify ➤ Freeze Transformations from the top menu.

The mech's right leg should now be a real object and no longer an instance. This can be confirmed by checking the leg meshes' scale XYZ values. In the Channel Box, the scale should be X = 1, Y = 1, and Z = 1. Make sure none are -1.

When you run the Instance to Object operation on your leg meshes, it may add a prefix to the legs, such as `char_mech_01_low_mech_r_femur`. These prefixes can be removed by following these steps:

1.  In the Outliner, expand `char_mech_01_low` to see the added prefixes.

2.  The name will appear as `char_mech_01_low_mech_r_tibia`. Double-click the names and remove `char_mech_01_low_`.

3.  This will leave the name `mech_r_tibia` for the tibia mesh.

4.  Make sure to make these name changes to the rest of the right leg (see Figure 7-3).

**Figure 7-3.** *Renamed right leg meshes*

Now you need to move the UVs of the right leg over to a neighboring quadrant (also referred to as a *tile*) so that they are not overlapping with the left leg in 0-to-1 space (U1, V1). To do that, follow these steps:

1. In Object Mode, hold Shift and select the mech_r_femur, mech_r_tibia, mech_r_foot, and mech_r_toe meshes.

2. Open the UV Editor (choose Windows ➤ Modeling Editors ➤ UV Editor).

3. Switch to UV Mode (right-click within the UV Editor). Press Ctrl+Shift+A (or marquee select over all shells) to select all the UVs.

4. In the UV Toolkit, under the Transform section, within Move, change the value to 1.000 (see Figure 7-4).

*Figure 7-4.* *Move UV selection*

5.  Select the right arrow to shift the UVs to the right one quadrant
    (see Figure 7-5).

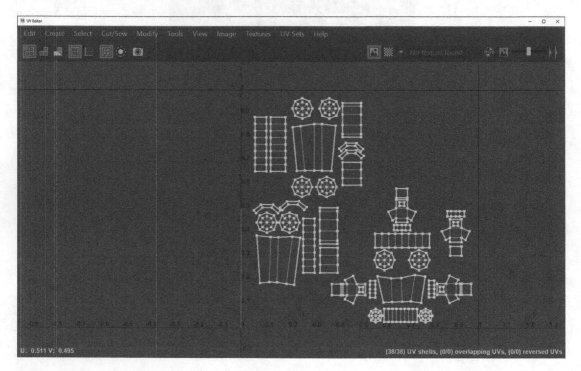

*Figure 7-5.* *UVs for the right leg selected*

6.  In the View Panel, while the right leg UVs are still selected, Shift-
    select the left legs as well. You should end up seeing both UVs in
    different quadrants (U1, V1 and U2, V1), as shown in Figure 7-6.

The main purpose of this last step is to show that the left and right leg UVs were
originally laying on top of each other and now one of them is moved out of the way and
sitting in its own UV tile. Therefore, it is okay if selecting meshes in UV Mode in the View
Panel is a little finicky. You can adjust them.

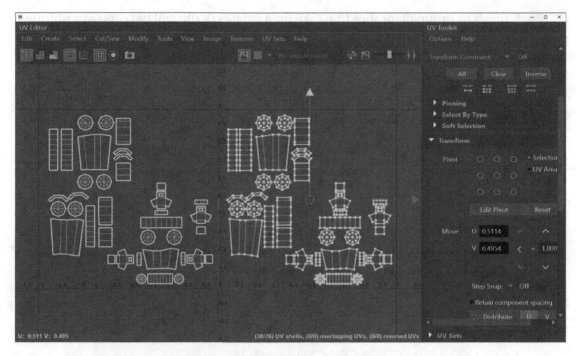

***Figure 7-6.*** *UVs for the selected left and right leg*

# Working with Multiple Textures on a Single Model

The head, body, and leg models are all currently using a single Maya material, a default Lambert material (`lambert1`). For the modeling pipeline, you only needed one material to view the model with. However, at a certain point during the texturing pipeline, you need to assign materials according to the UV layout of the model.

If you recall in Chapter 5, you laid out the UVs of the mech as follows:

> **U1, V1:** `mech_body` and `mech_head` together

> **U1, V1:** `mech_(l/r)_femur`, `mech_(l/r)_tibia`, `mech_(l/r)_foot`, `mech_(l/r)_toe`

To fit the UVs on a single UV tile (U1, V1) with a texel density of 512 and a 2048-pixel resolution map, you needed to split up the model in this way.

Each mesh or group of meshes that take up a single UV tile will have its own unique texture. For later steps in the texturing process, each material will represent a different texture. Therefore, you need two materials for the mech model:

**Material 1:** For the body and head meshes

**Material 2:** For the leg meshes (femur, tibia, foot, and toe)

Since you already have a default material assigned to the entire model, you need to change materials for one. Let's assign a new material to the head and body:

1.  In the View Panel, hold Shift and select mech_head and mech_body.

2.  With the meshes selected, hold right-click for a menu to pop up, then toward the bottom of this popup menu, choose Assign Favorite Material ➤ Lambert (see Figure 7-7).

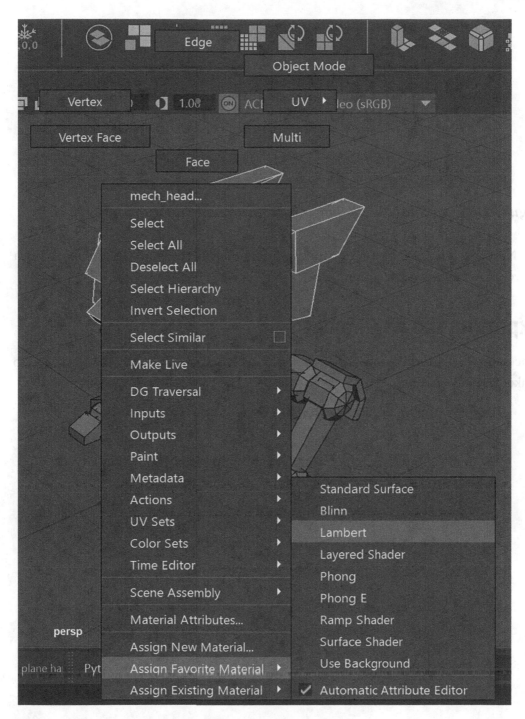

*Figure 7-7. The Assign Favorite Material menu option*

3.  Another Lambert material is applied to the body and head meshes.

4.  The Command Line (at the bottom of the Maya screen) will indicate that a Lambert shader was created and assigned to the selected objects (see Figure 7-8).

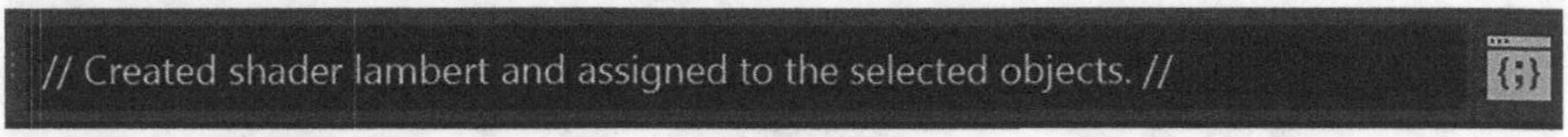

// Created shader lambert and assigned to the selected objects. //

*Figure 7-8.*  *Command Line showing a created Lambert material*

Now that you have the correct models assigned with their own materials, you can move on to exporting the model.

## Exporting the FBX Model

Since you will export the low and high res model with the FBX extension, you need to make sure it is enabled.

1.  In the top menu, choose Windows ➤ Settings/Preferences ➤ Plug-in Manager.

2.  In this Plug-in Manager, search for fbx and enable both Loaded and Auto load for gameFbxExporter.mll and fbxmaya.mll.

3.  Choose Close to exit from the Plug-in Manager window.

4.  Open the Outliner window if it is not yet open.

5.  In the top menu, choose Windows ➤ Outliner.

6.  In this Outliner window, select the char_mech_01_low group.

7.  With the group still selected, choose File ➤ Export Selection from the top menu.

The Export Selection window will open with options to the right. The settings should be set to the defaults if you have not modified them.

8. You can choose where you want to save the model and edit as follows:

   a. Filename: `char_mech_01_low`

   b. Files of Type: Fbx

   c. Choose Export Selection

9. Then, in the Outliner window, select the `char_mech_01_high` group.

10. Choose File ➤ Export Selection from the top menu again.

11. Repeat the Export Selection window steps for the high poly count model.

# Installing and Opening Substance 3D Painter

Download Substance 3D Painter from `www.substance3d.com` and install it. A free trial and educational versions are available. All the different licenses offer full features. You will need to create a new account with Substance to register the product. When you run the program the first time, you need to register the product's license following the prompts. I used Substance 3D Painter 2021 at the time of writing this book.

If you choose to add Substance's shortcut app to your desktop on installation, you can double-click the program's icon to start it. Substance can also be opened from the Windows Start menu ➤ Programs Files ➤ Adobe ➤ Adobe Substance 3D Painter, and on the Mac by choosing Applications ➤ Adobe ➤ Adobe Substance 3D Painter.

# Overview of the Substance 3D Painter Interface

Substance 3D Painter consists of several windows that can be dragged and repositioned. The interface (see Figure 7-9) includes a top menu, toolbar, layers, properties, Viewport, texture set, assets, and display settings. I briefly discuss the interface and explain it as needed throughout this chapter.

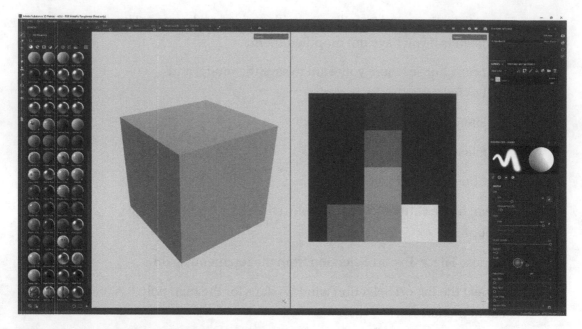

*Figure 7-9.* *Substance 3D Painter's interface*

# The Top Menu

The top menu shown in Figure 7-10 is the main menu that sits at the top of the Substance 3D Painter program window and provides access to all program's the basic functions.

File        Edit        Mode        Window        Viewport        Python        JavaScript        Help

*Figure 7-10.* *Top menu*

# The Toolbar

The main toolbar (see Figure 7-11), which is located at the top left, contains all the essential tools for painting when a paint layer is active such as Paint and Eraser. The secondary toolbar, located below the top menu, gives you access to settings to the currently selected tool, which you can modify.

*Figure 7-11.* *Toolbar*

# The Layers Panel

The Layers Panel (see Figure 7-12), like Photoshop's Layer Panel, allows you to create and modify a layer stack that contains paint strokes, fills, and effects. These layers will build the texture of the 3D object in the scene. In this panel, you can change the layer's order, group layers into folders, and adjust how layers blend between each other using blend modes and opacity.

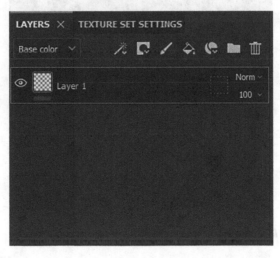

*Figure 7-12.* *Layers Panel*

# The Properties Panel

The Properties window (see Figure 7-13) lets you view and modify brushes, tools, and layer properties and parameters. The Properties window can be accessed by right-clicking in the Viewport.

***Figure 7-13.***  *Properties Panel*

## The Viewport

There are two Viewports in Substance 3D Painter (see Figure 7-14). Similar to Maya, the 3D view allows you to view your textured 3D mesh in 3D space, while the 2D view allows you to view the textured 2D layout of your mesh. Both views allow you to paint and texture your mesh and see it under different lighting conditions.

The bottom of the Viewport contains a computation bar that turns green to indicate when Painter is processing and computing tasks.

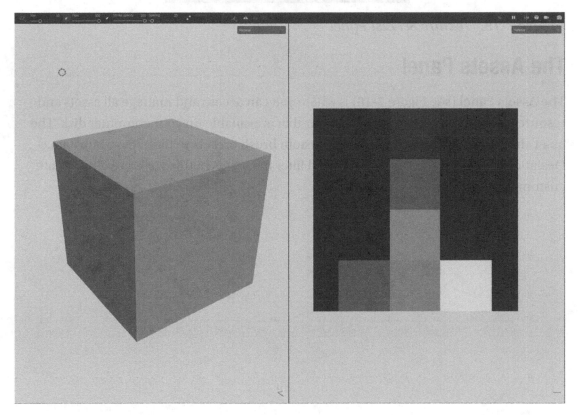

*Figure 7-14.*  *Viewport*

## The Texture Set List

The Texture Set List automatically displays all the material IDs associated with the imported mesh as texture sets. It will automatically populate with a new texture set (see Figure 7-15) when a new material is found. Each material ID must have unique UVs.

**Figure 7-15.** *Texture Set List Panel*

# The Assets Panel

The Assets Panel (see Figure 7-16) is where you can access and manage all assets and resources for a project, current session, or that is available on your computer disk. The asset shows various types of files from custom brush presets to bitmaps to Substance Designer materials. You can navigate and filter the assets in this view as well as create custom asset presets.

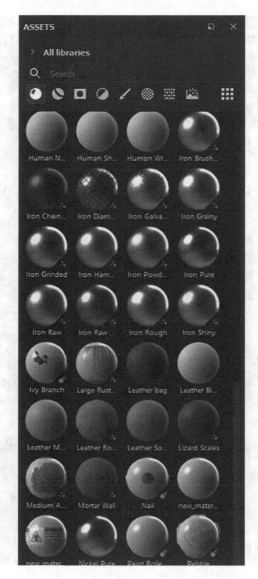

*Figure 7-16.* *Assets Panel*

# The Display Settings Panel

The Display Settings Panel (see Figure 7-17), located to the right of the program window, contains the environment, camera, and Viewport settings. Modifying these settings will affect the project and Viewport globally.

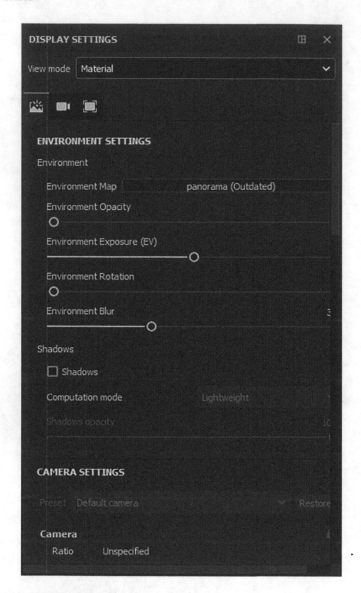

*Figure 7-17.* *Display Settings Panel*

# Preparing to Texture

In the following steps, you'll start by opening the low poly model that you have been working on throughout this book. You made both a low and high poly model in Chapters 3 and 6, but you only need to concern yourself with the low poly at this point.

1.  First, to make sure your UI within Painter looks the same, choose
    Window ➤ Reset UI in the top menu.

2.  Then choose File ➤ New. The New Project window will pop open.

3.  In this window, select from the Template dropdown menu, PBR–Metallic Roughness.

4.  Then, click the Select… button and load the `char_mech_01_low.fbx` file exported in the previous section. You can also use the starting project files labeled for this chapter.

5.  Change the document resolution to 2048.

6.  Change the Normal Map Format to OpenGL.

7.  Select OK to close the window.

The mech low poly model should have been loaded into the Viewport (see Figure 7-18). The Texture Set List should have been populated with the two Lambert materials you assigned to your model.

---

**Tip**    If you need to make additional modifications to your model that require you to replace it with a new one from Maya, there are additional steps to take. However, covering them is out of the scope of this book.

---

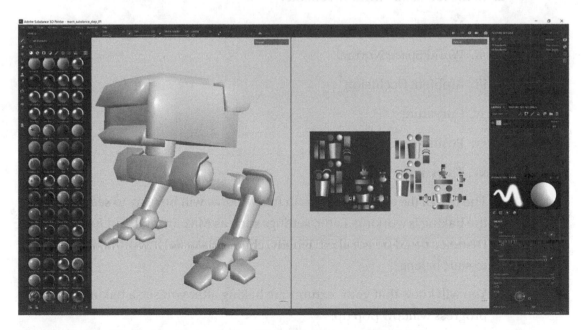

***Figure 7-18.*** *Untextured model inside of Substance 3D Painter*

Substance 3D Painter is like Maya in that the navigation tools work the same. To move around in the Viewport, hold Alt+left, middle, and right mouse clicks to rotate, pan, and zoom in and out. The one difference is that depending where you select with the mouse, the navigation will happen around that. In Maya, this navigation happens around the pivot of the model by default.

## Baking the Model

The next important part of the pipeline is to bake the texture maps.

1. Select the Texture Set Settings Panel. Then scroll down to the Mesh Maps section and choose Bake Mesh Maps.

2. In the Baking window that opened, change the Output Size to 2048.

3. Click the dog-eared page icon ▤ to the right of High-Definition Meshes and load the char_mech_01_high.fbx file.

4. Disable (check off) Use Low Poly Mesh as High Poly Mesh and switch Antialiasing to Subsampling 4x4.

    a. In the left of this window, enable:

        i. Normal

        ii. World Space Normal

        iii. Ambient Occlusion

        iv. Curvature

        v. Position

        vi. Thickness

    b. The rest of the default settings in this window will be okay to see if the baking is working. Later, settings such as Max Frontal and Rear Distance could be tweaked. Finally, choose Bake Selected Textures to start baking.

    c. You will know that your textures are baking after you see a baking progress window pop up.

    d. When the bar gets to 100%, click OK.

After the baking process occurs, you can inspect your mesh to see if there were any issues. Sometimes artifacts may appear. This happens for different reasons, such in areas where there may be missing or misprojected details on the geometry.

# Creating Textures Using a PBR Pipeline

The first thing you need to understand is that the materials (Lambert) you assign to your mech inside of Maya will be read as a texture sets within Substance 3D Painter. Additionally, you'll use texture maps, which include Base Color, Roughness, Metallic, Normal, and Height Map (see Figure 7-19). Within Substance 3D Painter, these texture maps will be represented as channels. These are the fundamental components known as Physically Based Rendering (PBR).

One of the main reasons we PBR is to achieve realistic materials, especially metals with physically accurate lighting properties. The other benefits include consistent lighting and a standardized set of values for visual artists and rendering programmers to adhere to.

> **Base Color:** The colors of the material, typically containing no lighting information.
>
> **Roughness:** Black to white values that make up how rough the surface of the material will be. Black represents smoothness (a glossy look) and white is rough (a matte look).
>
> **Metallic:** Black to white values that make up how metallic the surface of the material will be. 100% black represents non-metallic and 100% white represents metallic.
>
> **Normal:** RGB map, typically baked from the high poly to create the illusion of depth and more details.
>
> **Height:** Like the normal map, this is used to create the illusion of depth and more details. It is in grayscale as opposed to a normal map.

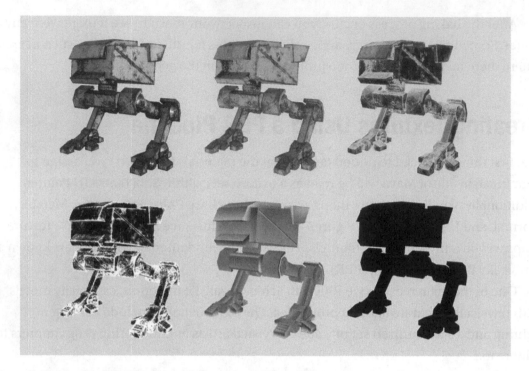

**Figure 7-19.** *Teddy Bear model material breakdown*

When you add paint by default on the mesh, you are essentially painting on all of these channels at the same time.

1.  In the Viewport, scroll through the different texture maps by pressing C.

2.  Go back to the overall material by pressing M.

3.  In the Properties window, scroll down and you will see the material section with its corresponding channels outlined in blue, as shown in Figure 7-20.

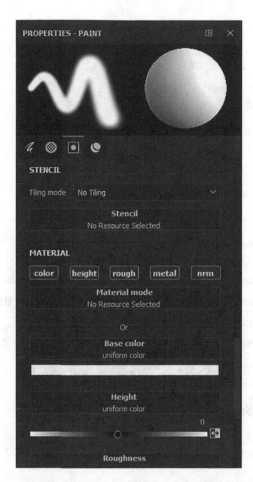

*Figure 7-20.* *Properties window showing a material's channels*

Deselect any blue outlined channel that you are not using. For instance, if you are only working on the color of the mesh, you would deselect the other channels.

## Starting to Texture

Let's begin to apply materials, masking, and alphas. The Layers panel will look as shown in Figure 7-21. In the next section, you will start to populate this panel.

***Figure 7-21.*** *Layers Panel with a blank layer*

1.  Next, in the Asset Panel, select the Smart Materials tab, the second icon from the left (see Figure 7-22). This will show all the Smart Materials that come with Substance.

***Figure 7-22.*** *Selected Smart Materials icon*

2.  Within the Assets Panel, search for Iron (see Figure 7-23).

***Figure 7-23.*** *Selected Iron Forged Old material*

3.  From the Materials Panel, hold a left-click, and drag the Iron Forged Old material over to the mech meshes:

    a. Once to the head or body (since they are both part of the same texture set).

    b. Repeat the last step for one of the legs (they are also part of the same texture set).

Make sure that the entire mech has this material.

4.  In the Asset Window, search for Machinery (see Figure 7-24).

**Figure 7-24.** *Searched Machinery material*

5.  From the materials panel, hold left-click, and drag the Machinery material over to the mech meshes:

    a.  Once to the head or body (since they are both part of the same texture set).

    b.  Repeat the last step for one of the legs (they are also part of the same texture set).

If you look at the Layers Panel, you can see the Iron Forged Old material underneath the Machinery one. By default, Painter adds a new material to the top.

# Masking

Substance 3D Painter heavily relies on masking for texturing. Layers will show only the specific areas of the texture based on the mask. You can utilize masking to add details such as scratches or wear and tear to the mech. You added a Smart Material, one on top of the other. Therefore, if you add a mask to the top material (Machinery), you will be able to see the material (Iron Forged Old) underneath.

In the Layers window, select the folder to the left of the Machinery material to expand its components (see Figure 7-25). This will show how the Machinery Smart Material is made.

As you gain more experience, you can add or edit the contents of the Smart Material or create your own from scratch.

***Figure 7-25.*** *Machinery's expanded components*

## Working with Smart Masks

Smart Masks can be made of a combination of generators, filters, or fill layers. Smart Masks can be dragged onto a layer. This is Painter's process of creating a generator. *Generators* are substances that create masks based on a model's Mesh Maps produced during the baking process. You can fine-tune these to affect the final mask's look.

1.  In the Asset Window, select the Smart Materials tab, the third icon
    from the left Smart Masks (see Figure 7-26). This will show all the
    Smart Masks that come with Substance.

***Figure 7-26.*** *Selected Smart Masks icon*

2.  In the Asset Window, search for Paint Subtle (see Figure 7-27).

***Figure 7-27.*** *Searched Paint Subtle Smart Mask*

3.  Hold Select and drag the Paint Subtle Smart Mask on top of the
    Machinery material layer in the Layers Panel.

The left square should now show the Machinery base color and the right square
should show the new Smart Mask.

The material knows where the edges are in order to add the edge wear look. This is calculated because the high poly was baked to the low poly. In this baking process, Substance 3D Painter calculated things such as the curvature of the model to establish where edges are at. For this reason, it was important to bake the high poly before working with these Smart Masks or Smart Materials.

4.  Select the mask square of the Machinery layer. This shows the Mask Editor sublayer (see Figure 7-28).

*Figure 7-28.* *Paint Subtle Smart Mask added to the Smart Material*

5.  Within this Paint Subtle mask, choose Mask Editor. In the Properties Panel, locate Global Balance and change it to 0.16 (see Figure 7-29).

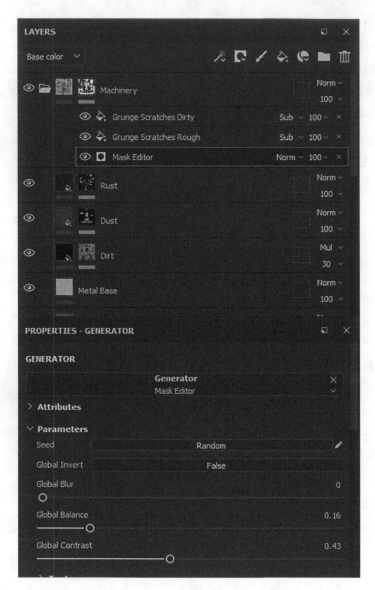

**Figure 7-29.**   *Global Balance within the Properties panel*

6. Within the Layers Panel and in the Machinery folder, locate the Rust layer.

7. Select the Rust mask. Then, choose Mask Editor and in the Properties Panel:

   a. Locate Global Balance and change it to 0.3.

b. Scroll down and choose Image inputs ➤ Texture (Secondary) ➤
   Parameters Section ➤ Seed. See Figure 7-30.

c. Then, to the left of Seed, select Random (until you find a grunge
   pattern you like).

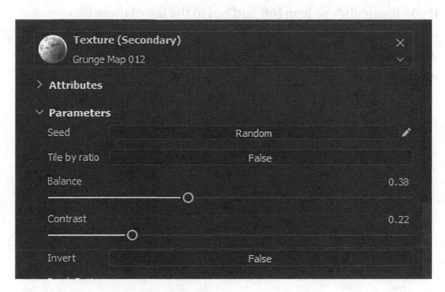

***Figure 7-30.*** *Texture (secondary)*

# Working with Multiple Materials

1. Make sure `lambert1` is selected in the Texture Set list
   (see Figure 7-31).

***Figure 7-31.*** *Selected lambert1 material*

2.  Double-click `lambert1` and rename it `mat_leg_01`
    (see Figure 7-32). *Mat* stands for material.

3.  Then, double-click `lambert2` and rename it `mat_body_01` (see
    Figure 7-32).

4.  If you toggle the eye icon (off and on) to the left of these two
    texture sets, the Viewport will show what material is attach to
    which parts of the body. This is to make sure that they are named
    properly (see Figure 7-32).

***Figure 7-32.*** *Renamed materials*

5.  Still in the Texture Set List, choose `mat_leg_01`.

In both the Viewport and Layers Panels, you should see the 3D mech showing the
newly added materials (see Figure 7-33).

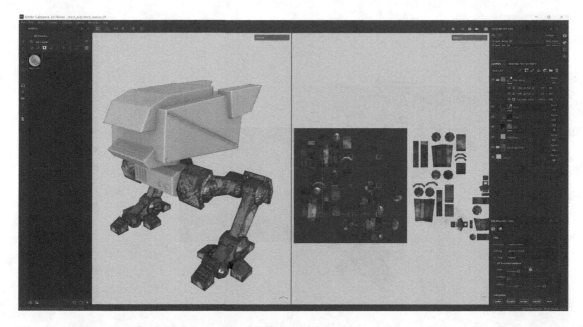

***Figure 7-33.*** *Mech_leg_01 newly added materials*

You can now copy the mech_leg_01 materials to mech_body_01. If for some reason materials were added to the body first, you can still do the following steps for the leg instead.

1.  In the Texture Set List, select mech_leg_01.

2.  Secondly, in the Layers Panel, select the folder icon to the left of the machinery to collapse it. Repeat this for Iron Forged Old.

3.  Still in the Layers Panel, hold Ctrl and select the Machinery and Iron Forged Olds layers. Then, press Ctrl+C (to copy them).

4.  Back to the Texture Set List, select the other texture set mat_body_01.

5.  Then back in the Layers Panel, hover over it and press Ctrl+V (to paste).

The materials should now be shown on both the body and the legs. In the Viewport Panel, the entire mech should now show the materials you added in the previous steps (see Figure 7-34).

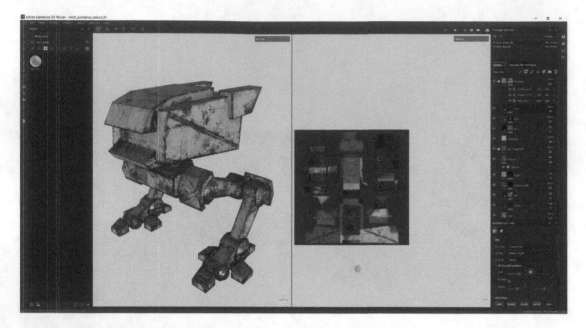

*Figure 7-34.* *Mech_body_01 with newly added materials*

## Adding Sticker Decals

Alphas provide a quick and precise way to add graphics to your textures. You can add iconography to the mech, which will help bring it more to life by giving it personality. First, you can add alphas that came with the book files:

1.  To import the alphas, from the top menu, choose File ➤ Import.

2.  The Import Resources window will open:

    a.  Click Add Resources and locate the Chapter 7 files:
        Decal_GeneralWarning_01.png.

    b.  Choose Undefined and change it to Alpha.

    c.  Change Import Resources to Project.

    d.  Lastly, choose Import.

3.  In the Texture Sets List, select mat_body_01 (or select mat_leg_01 if you want to add the decal to the legs).

4.  In the Assets Panel, select the Alphas Section icon (see Figure 7-35). Then, if you scroll through the alphas, you should see the imported image.

***Figure 7-35.*** *Selected Alphas icon*

5.  In the Layers Panel, select the Fill Layer icon ![icon] (to create a new fill layer). The decals will be added to this layer.

6.  In the Properties Panel, right-click the Base Color oversized button. Search for Decal_General (see Figure 7-36) in the popout window. Select the decal.

***Figure 7-36.*** *Searched Decal_GeneralWarning_01.png*

The decal will now show up as the base color (see Figure 7-37) and be shown in the Viewport (see Figure 7-38).

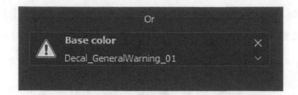

***Figure 7-37.*** *Oversized Base Color button*

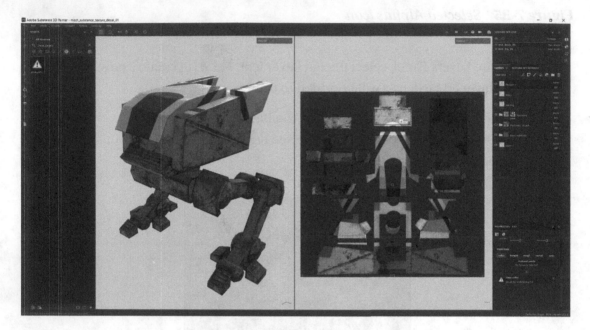

***Figure 7-38.*** *Large decal in the Viewport*

7. Still in the Fill Layer Properties panel:

   i. Deselect the Height, Rough, Metal, and Nrm buttons (they are outlined in light blue when enabled), since the decals should only output the color channel (texture maps).

   ii. Switch UV Wrap to None.

8. In the Viewport (2D section), use the decals transform manipulators to scale as desired (see Figure 7-39).

***Figure 7-39.*** *Resized warning decal*

9. To add more decals to the robot, create a new Fill layer and repeat the previous steps.

You should take this time to add as many images as possible to personalize your mech (see Figure 7-40).

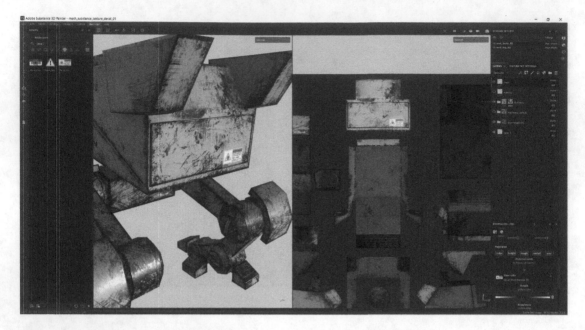

*Figure 7-40.* *Personalized mech*

You should now have your exported texture maps for the mech saved to your disk, ready for use in the chapters ahead.

## Exporting the Textures

To continue the game asset pipeline, you will export the textures from the final textured mech (see Figure 7-41). They will be added to the game engine in a later chapter.

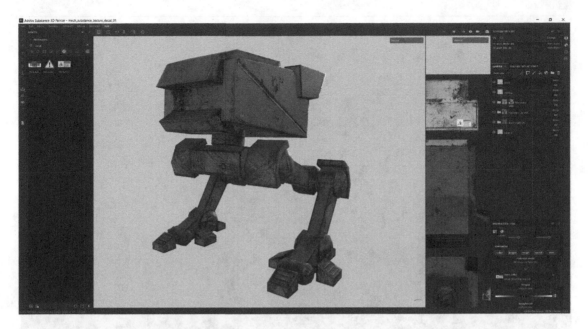

***Figure 7-41.*** *Final textured mech*

It is common practice to add the textures back to the 3D program you used to model to see if any changes need to be made before adding them to the game engine. To export the textures:

1.  In the top menu, choose File ➤ Export textures.

2.  Use Figure 7-42 for the rest of the steps under the General Export Parameters tab in the Settings tab. In the Export Textures window that opened:

    a.  Change the output directory to where you want to save the texture images.

    b.  In the Output template, choose PBR MetalRough.

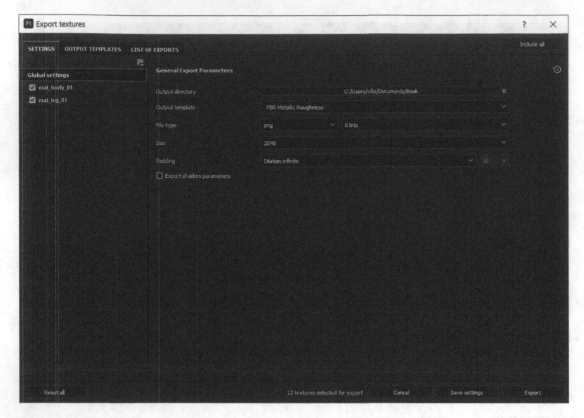

*Figure 7-42.*  *Export textures*

# Configuring Custom Output Texture Maps

In order for this template to align more with your needs, you need to modify it:

1.  Select the Output Templates tab to the right of the Settings tab. Here, you can configure and further customize texture export presets.

2.  In the Presets list to the left of the window, navigate to the PBR MetalRough preset and select it.

You should now see the configurations of the chosen preset's Output textures in the center Output Maps list (see Figure 7-43).

To the right is a list of Input Maps and Mesh Maps (Channels and Converted Textures) that are used to composite the content for the Output Maps.

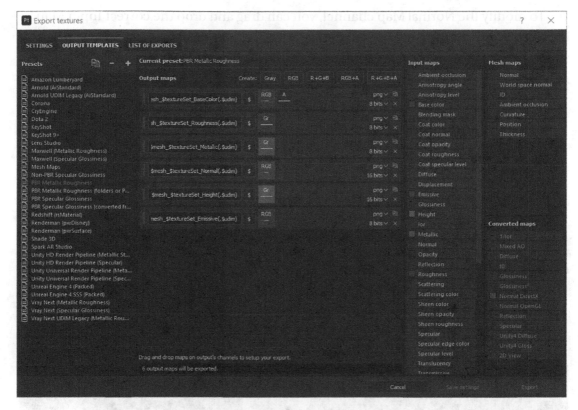

*Figure 7-43. Output Templates settings*

In the Output Maps section, you can see how the texture maps will be named and exported, as well as see the Input Maps that they consist of in their channel slots. Channel slots of an Output Map can be changed by dragging and dropping different Input Maps into the corresponding slots. If a color appears next to an Input Map on the left side of it, it means that it is assigned to a channel slot of one of the Output Maps of a matching color.

You only need to modify one channel slot, the Normal map. However, this texture configuration is good to know in case a project calls for customized texture Output Maps.

Currently with the chosen PBR MetalRough preset, the normal map is set to be compatible with DirectX graphics API. At the time of writing this book, Unity defaults to the OpenGL (graphics API). Depending on which one is used, this affects how game engines or 3D programs interpret the direction of the Y axis (green channel) of normal maps. Therefore, you need to modify the preset so that the normal map is compatible with OpenGL instead of DirectX. Otherwise, the normal map for the mech will be inverted when you take it into Unity.

To modify the Normal Map channel, you can drag and drop the correct Input Map into the Output Map channel slot to update it. In the following steps, the names may vary on your computer. The only thing you need to look out for is the ending of the maps' names. For example, normal maps always end with _Normal.

1.  In the right section under Converted Maps, choose Normal OpenGL and drag over to the Normal Output Map's RGB (see Figure 7-44) box 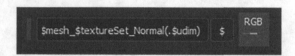.

*Figure 7-44.*  *Normal map channel*

2.  Then, in the popup menu, select RGB Channels (see Figure 7-45).

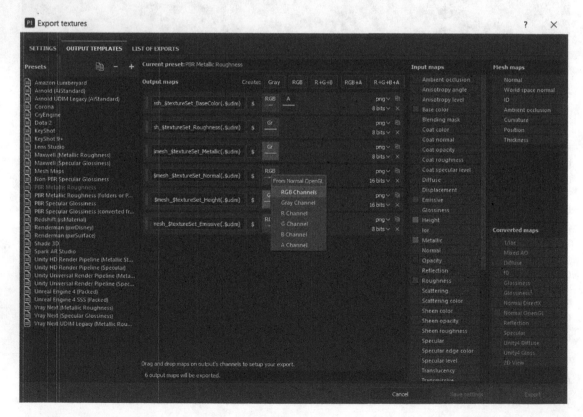

*Figure 7-45.*  *RGB Channel popup menu*

You should now see your Output Normal map's channel slot connected to the Normal OpenGL of the same color, as shown in Figure 7-46.

**Figure 7-46.**  *RGB Channel popup menu*

Still in the Export Textures window, go back to the Settings tab and choose Export (see Figure 7-47).

**Figure 7-47.**  *Export section*

The textures should now be exporting. They will be used in Chapter 9 when you set up your textures and materials in Unity.

# Summary

In this chapter, you first added floating details to the mech. Then, you baked your high poly down to your low poly to create a normal map. This gave you the necessary details to add edge wear. The chapter included an overview of Substance 3D Painter. You learned about the basic components of physically based rendering and how materials are broken down. Then, you utilized Smart Materials as a starting point to understand how masking works through layer order. Furthermore, you used alphas to customize the mech. The chapter finished by exporting the textures so they can be used by the game engine.

# CHAPTER 8

# Rigging the Mech

The mech you created so far is considered a character who usually will need to be animated. To allow for 3D animation on a mesh, you need to rig the mesh first. You need to think from an animator's perspective about the best way to manipulate mesh transformations. For this, you can create a rig. This example happens to be a character, but rigs can be made for all assets in games. Rigs are created by a technical animator. At this stage in the pipeline, the technical animator is in communication with the animator, to properly understand the demands of the rig. To create a rig, you will learn why a technical animator needs to communicate with the animator, as well as learn about working with joints, control curves, inverse kinematics, constraints, and grouping systems. See Figure 8-1.

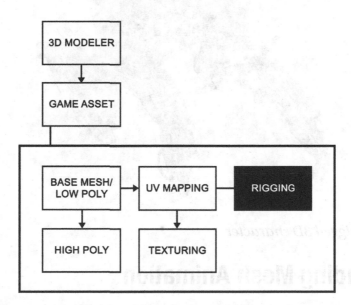

***Figure 8-1.*** *Flowchart of the rigging as part of the pipeline*

© Nova Villanueva 2022

N. Villanueva, *Beginning 3D Game Assets Development Pipeline*,
https://doi.org/10.1007/978-1-4842-7196-4_8

# What Is Rigging?

Rigging is the process of crafting controls for a mesh for the purpose to facilitating 3D animation of it (see Figure 8-2). Meshes can be rigged with methods that include binding, constraints, or procedural programming. An armature gets built with joints that hold meshes together, referred to as a skeleton in the industry. Then, these joints are easily moved by user interface looking controls. To correctly rig an asset, you must have an understanding of how it will later need to move. For instance, if you rig one robotic arm; when its hand is moved, it could also move the elbow like a real-life hand. The technical animator must create a system for the rig to do this. Since the technical animator may not have all the information on how the animation would occur, it is important to have constant communication with the animator. There are also animation principles that the technical animator needs to be aware of.

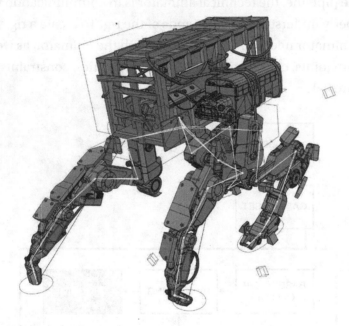

***Figure 8-2.*** *A rigged 3D character*

# Understanding Mesh Animation

Depending on the asset, which could be organic or hard surface in nature, different techniques can be used. For example, a mesh intended to have more organic deformation and movement like a human arm would have skin attached to it (known as a skin bind). On the other hand, a hard surface mesh that will move mechanically, such as a typewriter, might be constrained to a skeleton in a way that allows it to move with little to no organic deformation. A technical animator will complete a rig after choosing the best method for the asset.

However, a rig could be altered after the technical animator by another person on the team, such as a gameplay programmer. For instance, a procedural rig could adapt to the environment by positioning its feet on a sloped terrain. When you take a keyframe animation approach, which you will learn about in the next chapter, the movement will seem as if it were prerecorded. These two approaches can be combined in a game.

You read about how meshes held together by joints are necessary for animation. These joints are typically not zeroed out in their X, Y, and Z coordinates. What this means is that when animating them, it could make it hard for an animator to get an arm, for instance, to go back to its starting position. The joints could potentially have high numbers in the X, Y, and Z coordinates, which would cause it to take a long time to reset the rig back to default. For this reason, a rig uses controls that have zeroed transforms and are used to move the joints. Although this is a typical feature of rigs, it is one of the fundamental reasons that you need them.

## What Are Joints?

Joints act very similarly to how the human or animal skeletal system works. A hierarchical joint system connects joints with constraints or parenting, as shown in Figure 8-3. A child joint can freely move on its own unless its parent joint is moved. The parent will control the movement of the child. In Maya and other 3D programs, you can position the joints freely inside your meshes using the Translate tool (W).

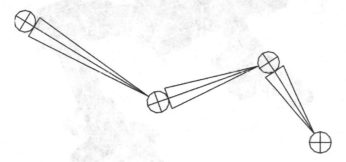

*Figure 8-3.* *Joints*

For the following steps, you can continue from the scene files you created in the previous chapter or open the start file named start_ch8.

1.   In the shelf tabs located above the Viewport, toggle to Rigging, as
     shown in Figure 8-4.

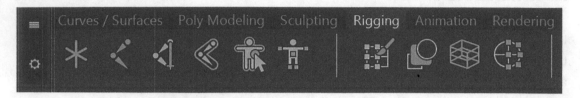

**Figure 8-4.** *Rigging toggle shelf tab*

# Working with Joints

You will be moving and positioning joints using the View Panels. If it is unclear which
camera you are viewing from, the Viewport shows the camera's name at the bottom.
If you are starting with the `start_ch8` provided with this book, you should be in persp
(perspective) view (see Figure 8-5).

**Figure 8-5.** *Perspective view of the mech*

1. If the Side View Panel is not already open, choose Panels ➤
   Orthographic ➤ Side (see Figure 8-6). The side view will end up
   looking like Figure 8-7.

---

**Tip**    While in a four-panel view layout, you can change quickly to one of the views
by hovering the mouse over the desired View Panel and tapping the spacebar. If you
are currently in a single View Panel, it switches to a four-panel view and vice versa.

---

***Figure 8-6.***  *Viewport Panels menu*

To create joints and easily move them around, you need to view them from
a side view.

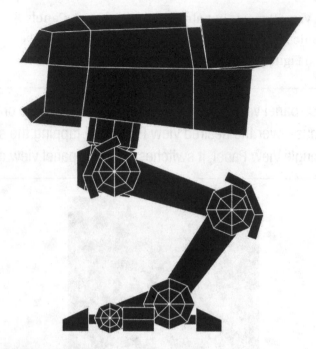

**Figure 8-7.** *Side view of the mech*

Before you create joints, you need to be able to see through your meshes:

1. Directly below the shelf, choose Shading ➤ X-Ray Joints (see Figure 8-8).

2. Make sure the Wireframe on Shaded is on by choosing Shading ➤ Wireframe on Shaded (or pressing Alt+5).

***Figure 8-8.*** *X-Ray Joints selected*

# Creating Joints

Joints are created in a hierarchical system. If you click once with the joint tool selected (see Figure 8-9), every click after that will automatically connect the new joint with the previous one. Next, assume that you have talked to an animator and have made note of their expectations for the mech's movements.

From the notes, you gather that the head will need to rotate along the Y axis. For the legs, let's draw inspiration from the Star Wars mechs, where the knees bend opposite from a human's. If you are both rigging and animating the mech, you can understand the advantages this brings.

1. Select the Joint Tool icon in the Rigging shelf (see Figure 8-9).

***Figure 8-9.*** *Circled joint icon*

2. With the Joint Tool selected, click the locations labeled 1-7 in the order, as shown in Figure 8-10.

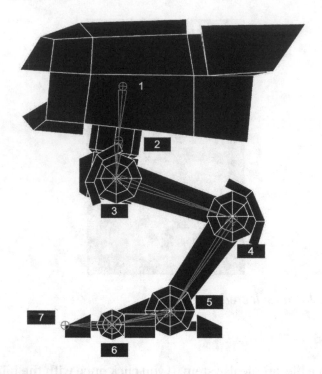

***Figure 8-10.*** *Joint system labelled 1-7*

If you need to delete joints, they can be removed by selecting them and clicking Delete. If needed, you can use Ctrl+Z to go back in case you need to make the joints again.

3.  Switch to the perspective view window by choosing Panels ➤ Perspective ➤ Persp. The perspective view will end up looking like Figure 8-11.

***Figure 8-11.*** *Perspective view of the joints*

The joints (see Figure 8-11) would have been created along the center of the grid unless you pressed V to snap the joints to the vertices on the mesh. Next, you need to rename them. It is industry standard to name the joints in the same fashion and reasoning as you did the meshes. There could be instances in a game where a weapon is attached to a particular joint, such as on a character's hand. Therefore, it helps to have everything named logically. Let's rename the first joint created atop:

1. If the Outliner window is not open, choose Windows ➤ Outliner from the top menu.

2. In this Outliner, expand all the joints by selecting the + icon to the left of them. The result will look as shown in Figure 8-12.

---

**Tip**   Select the +/- icon while holding Shift to expand/collapse the entire group hierarchy at once.

---

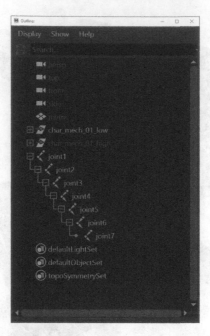

*Figure 8-12.*  *Expanded joints showing their hierarchy*

---

**Note**    If you deleted or undid the joints, the new joints may not be named the same as in Figure 8-12. This does not matter, as you will rename them.

---

3.  Still in the Outliner, select the first joint and double-click it to rename it. Name it jnt_head. When this one is selected, the perspective view should show that the joint of the head is selected (highlighted with a different color).

2.  Use the same naming convention to name the rest, as shown in Figure 8-13. Use _l_ to represent the *left* leg since you will be moving these joints later to use for the right side. Here's a guideline for all the joints:

    a. jnt_head

    b. jnt_root

    c. jnt_l_femur

    d. jnt_l_knee

e. jnt_l_ankle

f. jnt_l_ball

g. jnt_l_toe

***Figure 8-13.*** *Renamed joints*

## Arranging Joints

The joints will have to be arranged correctly. When an asset is animated, usually it will have a center of mass and gravity. This principle is associated with real science. With this in mind, you want the animator to be able to select this center and, from there, the rest of the joints could follow. In this case, this should be the root. The root usually ends up being in such a location. However, right now the head joint is not a child of the root. You need to fix this.

1. In the Outliner, select **jnt_root** and press Shift+P to unparent this joint from jnt_head (see Figure 8-14).

**Figure 8-14.**  *Unparent jnt_root joint*

The joint called jnt_root, along with its children, will be detached from jnt_head (see Figure 8-14).

2.  Select jnt_head, hold Ctrl, and select jnt_root, then press P to parent them.

3.  In the Outliner, expand the joints if needed to see them all, as shown in Figure 8-15.

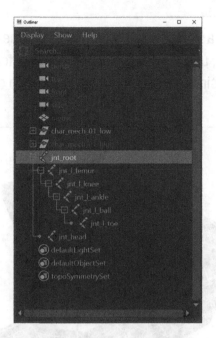

***Figure 8-15.*** *Joints acting as children to the root joint*

---

**Note**    What you select first becomes the child when using P to parent.

---

## Moving Joints

The joints are still at the center of the grid, as seen from the perspective view. Let's position the left foot joints in the correct location. Due to various complications that could later arise, keeping joints straight and not rotating them while positioning them will save a lot of potential trouble. As you move the joints, you should only translate them on the X, Y, and Z axes.

1. Still in the Outliner, select jnt_l_femur and press W to activate the Move tool.

2. In the perspective view, while holding V (to snap to vertices), move the joint called jnt_l_femur to snap to the corresponding vertex, as illustrated in Figure 8-16.

**Note**    To snap a joint to a vertex using the V hotkey, rather than using the translate arrows to move, use the center of the manipulator handle to quickly move and snap to the desired vertex. Zooming in helps to see if the snapping was successful.

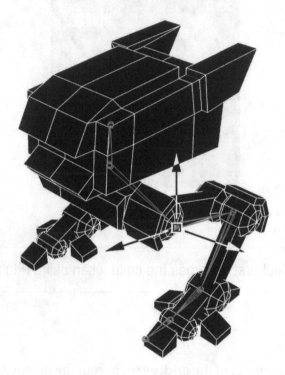

***Figure 8-16.***   *The femur joint pivot snapped to a vertex*

3.  Make sure the pivot of the joint is snapped exactly where the vertex is shown in Figure 8-17. It should appear in the center of the motor unit from the side view, but on the outward vertex from the perspective view. The entire femur will later rotate from this pivot.

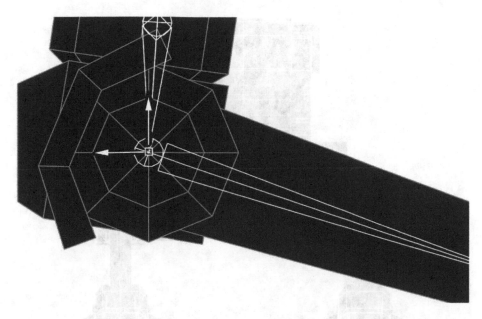

***Figure 8-17.*** *Pivot center of a joint snapped to vertex*

4.  With `jnt_l_femur` selected, translate on the Z axis (this could
    be different in your scene) for the purpose of keeping the axis
    location from the previous step. Translate the joint so that it
    snaps and sits in the center of the bottom part of the leg mesh, as
    illustrated in Figure 8-18.

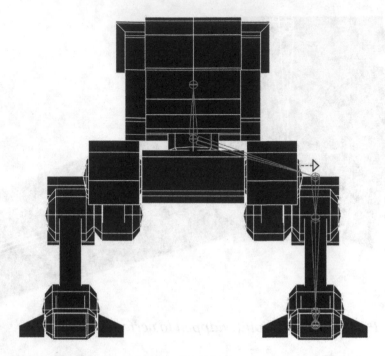

***Figure 8-18.*** *The femur joint translated in the Z axis*

Similarly to the way that the femur's joint was snapped to its corresponding motor unit, you can now work on the knee and ball joints:

1. Still in the Outliner, select jnt_l_knee and press W to activate the Move tool.

2. In the perspective view, while holding V (to snap to vertices), move the joint called jnt_l_knee to snap to the center vertex of the mech_l_tibia's motor unit (see Figure 8-19).

3. Lastly, snap jnt_l_ankle and jnt_l_ball to their corresponding motor unit's vertex (see Figure 8-19).

The joints of the left leg should look like Figure 8-19. The knee, ankle, and ball should be snapped to the exterior part of the motor units.

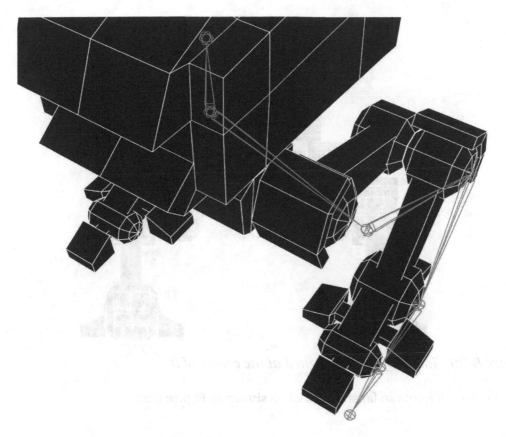

**Figure 8-19.**  *Snapped joints to outward vertices*

4.  With jnt_l_knee selected, translate (W) on the Z axis (this could
    be different in your scene) so it sits in the center of the bottom part
    of the mesh, as illustrated in Figures 8-20 and 8-21.

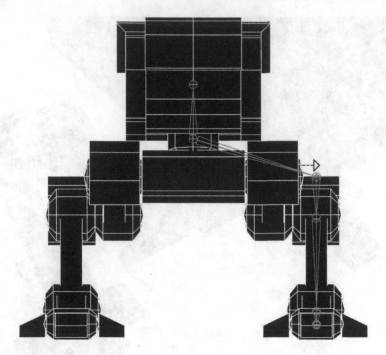

**Figure 8-20.** *Joints of the leg aligned at the center of it*

The overall joints so far should look as shown in Figure 8-21.

**Figure 8-21.** *Joints system*

# Mirroring Joints

You can use both the naming conventions and the positioning of the left leg to create the right side's joints. Be aware that this works best for symmetrical meshes. To speed up the process, Maya allows you to mirror joints from one side to the other. Similar to mirroring meshes, mirroring joints happens when the software duplicates them and reverses them across a defined axis. During this process, the duplicated joints can be renamed as well. You can specify their names by using the search and replace options. Follow the next steps to mirror the left leg:

1. On the left side and above the shelf tabs, switch the dropdown menu to Rigging (see Figure 8-22).

***Figure 8-22.***  *Dropdown menu set to Rigging*

2. From the Outliner or the perspective view, select jnt_l_femur.

3. With jnt_l_femur selected, choose Skeleton ➤ Mirror Joints ➤ Options Box □ from the top menu.

The Mirror Joints Options window will open (see Figure 8-23).

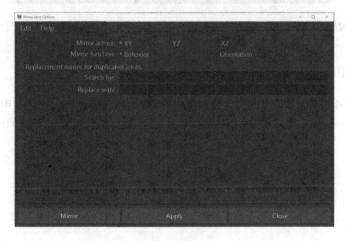

***Figure 8-23.***  *Mirror Joints Options window*

4. In this window, choose Edit ➤ Reset Settings to make sure your
   settings are the same.

In this window, apply the settings as shown in Figure 8-24:

5. Change XY to YZ for Mirror Across unless your joints need to be
   mirrored across a different axis. If you are not sure which access to
   mirror in, you can always apply the mirror, and then press Ctrl+Z
   to undo.

6. In the Replacement Names for Duplicate Joints option, Search For
   should be _l_. If you recall, you used _l_ earlier in the joint naming
   conventions. Replace With should be _r_ (see Figure 8-24).

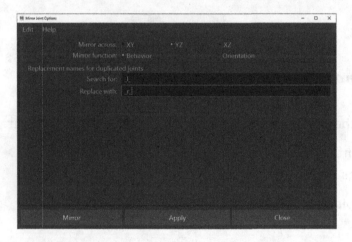

***Figure 8-24.*** *Settings for the Mirror Joints Options window*

7. Click Mirror.

The joints should end up mirrored, as shown in Figure 8-25. If they are not mirrored
across the intended axis, this is where you can undo the action (Ctrl+Z) and repeat from
the last step.

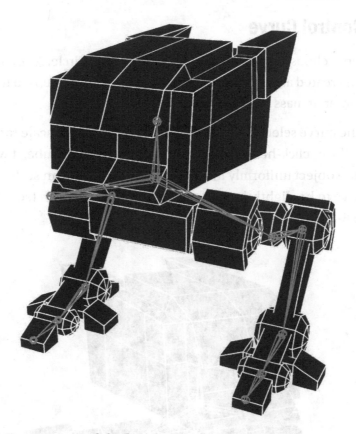

***Figure 8-25.***  *Mirror joints of the leg*

# Working with Control Curves

Now that you have joints, you need a way for the animator to be able to control them. Yes, the animator could simply select the joints and move them, but this is inconvenient. For example, if X = -283494, Y = 67839.046, and Z = 18273, this would end up causing more work on the animator's end to manually get them back to a default position.

Instead, you can facilitate the animator's job by creating controls that are made up of curves. The difference between joints and curves is that after they are positioned, curves can have their transform coordinates zeroed out. Then, the animator can use the zeroed (0, 0, 0) coordinates to bring the asset back to a default position. Since an asset is made up of multiple controls, having the animator remember large numbers is not efficient.

# Creating a Control Curve

From the top menu, choose Create ➤ NURBS Primitives ➤ Circle. A circular curve should have been created at the center of the grid. Follow these steps to turn it into the control for the center of mass of your asset:

1. With the curve selected, press R (scale tool). With the scale tool active, if you click-hold and drag out from the center cube, it will scale the object uniformly in all axes. This way, you can scale the curve to be slightly larger than the body of the mech (see Figure 8-26).

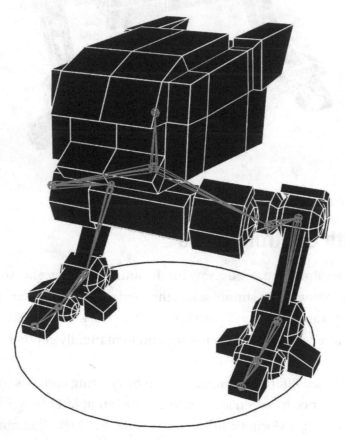

***Figure 8-26.*** *Resized circle curve*

Then, you need to make sure that the control curve's pivot, which should be at its center, is directly aligned with the joint's pivot that you are going to control. To do this, you will snap the curve to the joint. Do not worry if the following steps take a while, since the process of snapping curves to joints takes time and practice.

1. With the circle curve selected, press W (Translate Mode).

2. Hold V (snap tool) and drag to snap it to jnt_root (see Figure 8-27).

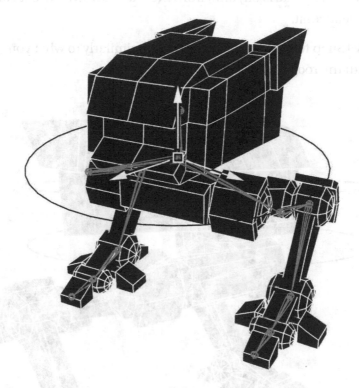

***Figure 8-27.*** *The curve's pivot on top of the root joint*

---

**Note**    Make sure the curve's pivot is right where the joint is. If it's not, the control may not work properly. Zoom in if you have to see it clearly.

---

3. In the Outliner, double-click the new curve called nurbsCircle1 and rename it ctrl_root.

4.  With `ctrl_root` selected, press Ctrl+D to duplicate it. In the perspective window, you will not see the duplicate because it is laying right on top of the other curve. Instead, you can see the duplicate in the Outliner.

5.  In the Outliner, double-click the second curve named `ctrl_root1` and rename it `ctrl_head`.

6.  With `ctrl_head` selected in the Outliner, press W (to make sure the Translate Mode is on) and, from the Y axis arrow, move it close to the head joint.

7.  Hold V (Snap tool) to snap it to `jnt_head`, similarly to what you did with the root joint (see Figure 8-28).

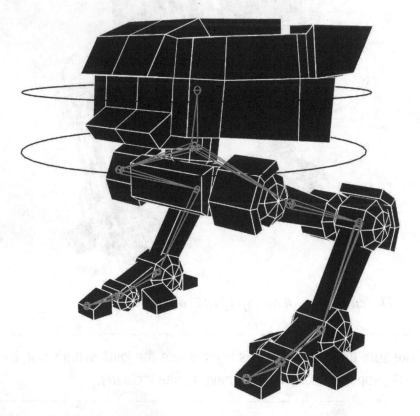

***Figure 8-28.*** *Curve's pivot on top of the root joint*

**Note**    To verify the control curve's placement is correct, navigate around in the scene in perspective view.

## Editing a Curve's Control Vertices

It is good practice to shape the control curves in a way that they wrap around and loosely conform to the shape they are controlling. Having a rig with a good interface design makes it easily recognizable to the animator. For most of the rig, the animator should be able to look at a controller and know exactly what mesh it controls. Let's shape the head curve to fit the head mesh of the mech with the following steps:

1.  In the perspective view, with `ctrl_head` selected and while hovering over the curve or in the empty space, hold the right-click and (after the hotbox menu pops up) drag to the left to the Control Vertex button.

In Control Vertex Mode, you should see points on the curve. This mode lets you edit the curve. These points can be translated (W), rotated (E), and scaled (R). However, if you need to move the entire curve, you can go back to Object Mode in the same way, by holding right-click and dragging over to Object Mode.

The idea is that you can go back and forth depending on what you need to do. When you do this, keep in mind that the pivot of the curve (where the curve will rotate from) needs to be at the location of the joint it is controlling. This change only happens in Object Mode. Vertex Mode will keep the pivot location where it is. You already snapped the curve to the joint using Object Mode. Now you can freely move the vertices around the curve to shape it.

2.  With the Control Vertex Mode, select (left-click) vertex points from this control head curve and then press W to enable the Move tool.

3.  Translate the points to wrap around the head mesh, as Figure 8-29 shows.

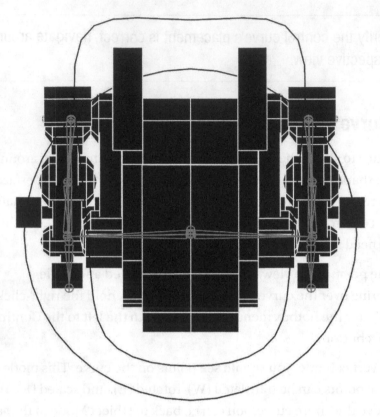

***Figure 8-29.*** *A curve wrapped around the head*

## Curve's Object Mode

1. With `ctrl_head` still selected, hold right-click and (after the
   hotbox menu pops up) drag over to the right to the Object Mode
   button.

The curve will highlight when in Object Mode. This is when you check again to make
sure the pivot of the curve is positioned where the joint is (see Figure 8-30). If it is not,
you can snap it (V) to the joint, as you did in a previous exercise.

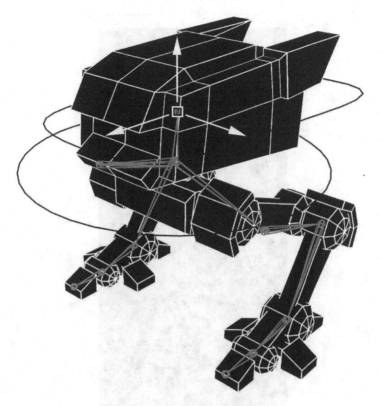

***Figure 8-30.*** *Selected head's control curve in Object Mode*

Still with `ctrl_head` selected:

2.   Press Alt+Shift+D (to delete the history from the curve).

3.   Choose Modify ➤ Freeze Transformations.

As a review, freezing transformations will hold the location of the mesh or curve and set all of its transformations on the X, Y, and Z axes to 0 for translation and rotation and 1 for scale. As you may recall, having a way for the animator to easily reset the location of the controls (of the meshes) to their defaults makes things easier. With the head curve selected, if you look at the Channel Box (choose Windows ➤ General Editors ➤ Channel Box), all the transformations should now be frozen (see Figure 8-31).

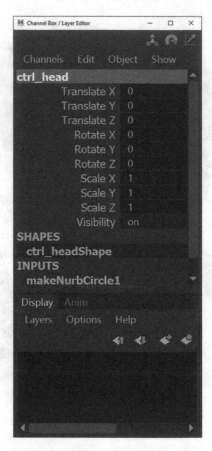

***Figure 8-31.*** *Channel Box showing freeze transformed coordinates*

Let's do the same to the root control curve. With `ctrl_root` selected:

1.  Press Alt+Shift+D (to delete the history from the curve).

2.  Choose Modify ➤ Freeze Transformations.

---

**Note**    You can perform the Delete History and Freeze Transformation operations on multiple curves and meshes by selecting one curve or mesh and then Shift-selecting another.

---

## Creating Feet Controls

The feet controls should be created similarly to the head's control. First, you will make the left side:

1.  From the top menu, choose Create ➤ NURBS Primitives ➤ Circle.

2.  With the newly created curve selected, press R (Scale tool). With the Scale tool active, scale the curve to be slightly larger than the foot of the mech.

3.  In the Outliner, double-click this new curve called nurbsCircle1 and rename it ctrl_l_foot.

4.  With ctrl_l_foot selected, press W (the Move tool).

5.  Hold V to snap it to jnt_l_ankle, similar to what you did with the head joint (see Figure 8-32).

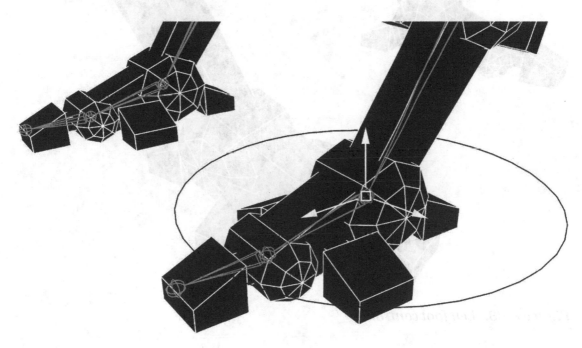

***Figure 8-32.*** *Left foot control*

Before you enable Vertex Mode to edit the curve, you can hide all the joints so that you do not accidently select them. When you need to snap to further joints, you can unhide the joints.

6. In the Outliner, select jnt_root and press Ctrl+H (to hide it).

7. In the perspective view, with ctrl_l_foot selected and while hovering over the curve or empty space, hold right-click and (after the hotbox menu pops up) drag over to the left to the Control Vertex button.

8. With the Control Vertex Mode, hold-select and drag outside of the foot curve to create a rectangle selection over all the vertex points. Then, let go. All the vertex points of this curve should now be selected (see Figure 8-33).

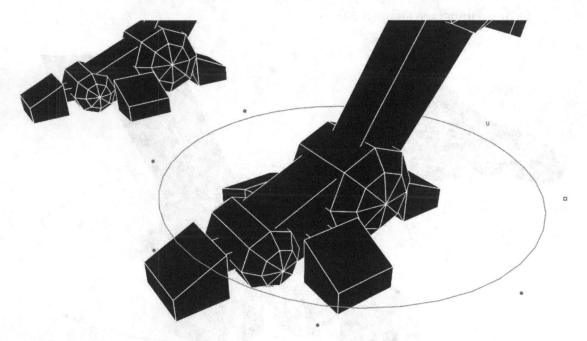

***Figure 8-33.*** *Left foot control*

9. Press W to enable translation of the vertex points.

10. Hold X (snap to grid), select-hold the arrow along the Y axis, and move it downward until it snaps to the grid, as shown in Figure 8-34.

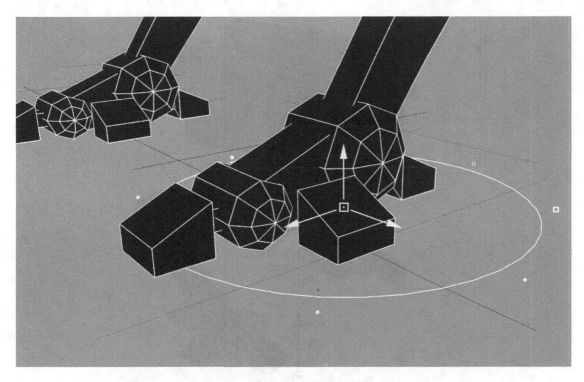

***Figure 8-34.*** *Left foot control snapped to the ground*

11. Then, select and translate the points to wrap around the left foot mesh (see Figure 8-35), as you did the head control.

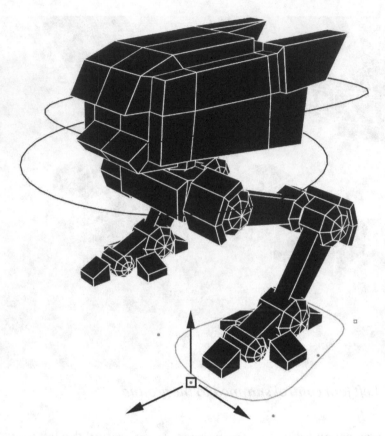

**Figure 8-35.**  *Left foot shaped control curve*

12.  With `ctrl_l_foot` still selected, hold right-click and (after the
     hotbox menu pops up) drag over to the left to the Object Mode
     button.

By moving the vertex points only, you can see that the pivot of the left foot control
is still positioned where the ankle joint is. You can only see this from Object Mode
(see Figure 8-36). The animator will be able to rotate the foot from this ankle position,
similarly to how a human foot rotates.

**Figure 8-36.** *Left foot shaped control curve*

13. In the Outliner, select `jnt_root` and press Shift+H (to unhide it).

14. With `ctrl_l_foot` selected, press Ctrl+G (to create a group from it). This group will only be visible in the Outliner.

15. From the Outliner, with `group1` selected, press Ctrl+D (to duplicate it).

16. With `group2` still selected, in the Channel Box, change the scale X to -1 (see Figure 8-37).

**Figure 8-37.** *Channel Box showing group2 transforms*

17. Hold Shift and select group1. Now, with both groups selected, choose Edit ➤ Ungroup from the top menu.

18. In the Outliner, rename ctrl_l_foot1 to ctrl_r_foot.

19. Hold-Shift and select ctrl_l_foot and ctrl_r_foot, then press Alt+Shift+D (to delete the history from the curve).

20. With these leg controls still selected, choose Modify ➤ Freeze Transformations from the top menu.

## Creating Knee Controls

Lastly, you will create knee controls. When moving and animating the legs of a 3D character, the knees can sometimes behave unpredictably or oddly. Therefore, having knee controls is beneficial.

1. From the top menu, choose Create ➤ NURBS Primitives ➤ Circle.

2. With the newly created curve selected, press R (Scale tool). With the Scale tool active, scale the curve to be approximately the size shown in Figure 8-38.

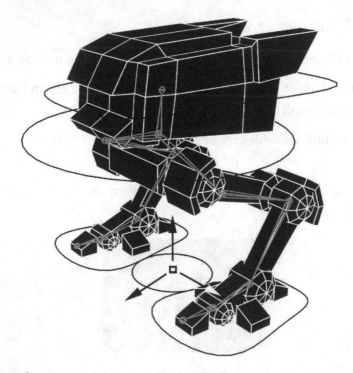

*Figure 8-38.* Circle curve scaled

256

3.  In the Outliner, double-click the new curve called `nurbsCircle1` and rename it `ctrl_l_knee`.

4.  With `ctrl_l_knee` selected, press W (Move tool) if it is not active.

5.  Hold V and snap it to `jnt_l_knee` (see Figure 8-39).

***Figure 8-39.*** *Left knee control selected*

6.  In the Channel Box, change the value in Rotate X to 90 so the
    control looks like Figure 8-40.

***Figure 8-40.*** *Left knee control rotated by 90 degrees*

7. Select the arrow along the Z axis and move the control away from the mesh, as shown in Figure 8-41.

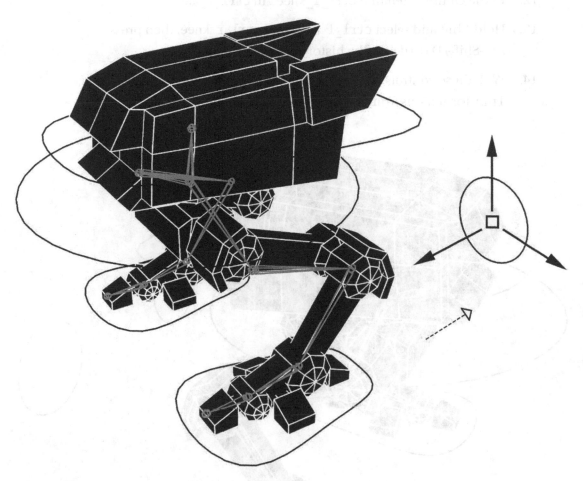

***Figure 8-41.*** *Left knee control positioned away from the leg mesh*

8. With `ctrl_l_knee` selected, press Ctrl+G (to create a group from it). This group will only be visible in the Outliner.

9. From the Outliner, with `group1` selected, press Ctrl+D (to duplicate it).

10. With `group2` still selected, in the Channel Box, change Scale X to -1. Then choose Edit ➤ Ungroup from the top menu (see Figure 8-42).

11.   Select group1, and in the same way as the previous step, choose
      Edit ➤ Ungroup.

12.   In the Outliner, rename ctrl_l_knee1 to ctrl_r_knee.

13.   Hold-Shift and select ctrl_l_knee and ctrl_r_knee, then press
      Alt+Shift+D (to delete the history from the curve).

14.   With these controls still selected, choose Modify ➤ Freeze
      Transformations from the top menu.

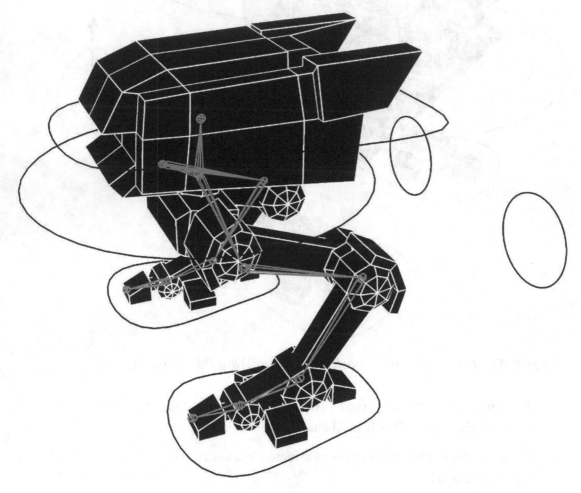

*Figure 8-42.* *Knee controls*

# Using Kinematics for Movement

A rig can use Forward Kinematics (FK), Inverse Kinematics (IK), or a combination to switch back and forth between them. In an FK setup, the movements happen in child-to-parent chained joints, where each of the bones are rotated individually. On the other hand, in an IK setup, a target (usually a foot or hand) is positioned and an IK solver determines where the rest of the bones will end up. An FK setup may provide an animator with more accurate poses, but it takes longer to animate. An IK setup may provide less control over poses but is quicker to animate. It is good to have an understanding of both of these methods. You can rig the mech you are making with an IK setup for the legs.

## Creating IKs for the Legs

1. In the Outliner, expand all the joints (see Figure 8-43).

**Figure 8-43.** *The Outliner shows an expanded joint chain*

2. In the Rigging shelf tab, select the IK ◁ icon.

3. With the IK tool active and in the View Panel, first select jnt_l_femur and then jnt_l_ankle.

4. The Outliner should now show both an effector1 and an ikHandle1 (see Figure 8-44).

5. Double-click ikHandle1 and rename it IK_l_leg.

6. Repeat these IK steps for the right leg, renaming the IK to IK_r_leg.

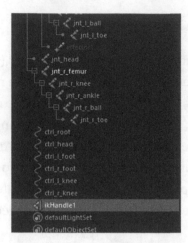

***Figure 8-44.*** *The Outliner shows an effector and iKHandle*

You can now test the IK handle to see if it set up properly:

1. In the Outliner, select IK_l_leg.

2. Back in the View Panel, press W (Move tool).

3. While selecting the center of the manipulator handle, hold-select and drag it around to see the ankle move and see the joints follow accordingly.

4. Lastly, do not forget to press Ctrl+Z to undo the changes and revert back to the original rig without the test translations to the IK handle.

# Connecting Vector Poles for the Knees

1. In the top left area of Maya, switch the Menu Set dropdown to Rigging or press F3 (see Figure 8-45).

***Figure 8-45.*** *Rigging menu set*

2. In the Outliner, first select ctrl_l_knee then hold Ctrl and select IK_l_leg.

3.   Then, from the top menu, choose Constrain ➤ Pole Vector.

4.   Repeat the same for the right side: select ctrl_r_knee then
     hold Ctrl and select IK_r_leg. Then, from the top menu, choose
     Constrain ➤ Pole Vector.

***Figure 8-46.*** *IK with pole vectors*

# What Are Constraints?

Constraints force the position, orientation, or scale of an object onto others. If, for
instance, the mech's head is constrained to the head control curve, when the control
rotates, these transform values will be passed down to the head mesh, making it rotate as
well. In Maya, you select one object followed by the one that needs to be controlled, then
add the constraint to it. You need to add several constraints to your meshes and controls
in this project in order for this rig to be completed.

# The Importance of Using Constraints

Controls are useless without being able to control the meshes. You can use a constraint
method to achieve full control. It is a common mistake for beginners to try to parent
meshes to joints in order to combine everything. On the contrary, joints should be
kept separate from the meshes. In terms of efficiency, it becomes a mess in a game
engine when you have an entire character with a long joint chain and you are trying to
determine where a backpack asset ended up. From a technical standpoint, if you need
to make changes to the rig, a lot of problems will likely develop. Hence, you can use
constraints instead.

For hard surface meshes such as the mech, the key is to add constraints to groups
containing meshes instead of a direct connection to the meshes. In this way, if the art
needs to be changed, this setup will allow for it. As mentioned in previous chapters, the
3D pipeline is nonlinear. Based on a lead or director's feedback, you may have to make
future changes to the assets you create. Therefore, you need flexible workflows that will
support these changes.

# Creating Groups

In this section, you will work only with the low poly meshes. To do so, follow these steps:

1. Expand char_mech_01_low to see all the meshes in the group (see Figure 8-47).

**Figure 8-47.** *Outliner showing expanded mech's low poly meshes*

2. Still in the Outliner, select mech_head and press Ctrl+G (to group it).

3. Double-click this newly created group and rename it mech_head_grp.

4.  Repeat the last two steps with the rest of the meshes until you get to the head, renaming the groups to mech_body_grp, mech_r_femurgrp, mech_r_foot_grp, mech_r_tibia_grp, mech_r_toe_grp, mech_l_femur_grp, mech_l_tibia_grp, mech_l_foot_grp, and mech_l_toe_grp (see Figure 8-48).

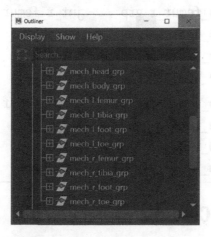

***Figure 8-48.***  *Low poly mesh groups*

Each group's pivot needs to be positioned at the location of its corresponding pivot. For this you have to enable Pivot Mode and snap its transform to the joint:

1.  Still in the Outliner, select mech_head_grp and press W (to enable Transform). Then press D (to enable the movement of its pivot).

2.  Hold V to snap this pivot location to the head joint (jnt_head). Then, press D again to disable the pivot access.

3.  Repeat the previous two steps, but use Table 8-1 as a guide to placing the pivot.

**Table 8-1.** *Meshes Pivot Locations*

| Mesh Group | Snap to Joint |
|---|---|
| mech_head_grp | jnt_head |
| mech_body_grp | jnt_root |
| mech_femur_r_grp | jnt_r_femur |
| mech_foot_r_grp | jnt_r_ball |
| mech_tibia_r_grp | jnt_r_knee |
| mech_toe_r_grp | jnt_r_toe |
| mech_femur_l_grp | jnt_l_femur |
| mech_foot_l_grp | jnt_l_ball |
| mech_tibia_l_grp | jnt_l_knee |
| mech_toe_l_grp | jnt_l_toe |

## Setting Up the Head Control

You need the head to rotate side to side from its pivot origin.

1. In the Outliner, expand all the joints until they are all visible.

2. In the Outliner, first select jnt_head then hold Ctrl and select mech_head_grp. Choose Constrain ➤ Parent from the top menu.

In the Channel Box, mech_head_grp will have light blue boxes (see Figure 8-49), which indicate that the Translate and Rotate attributes are being constrained.

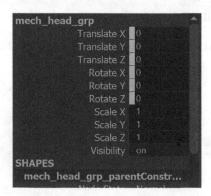

**Figure 8-49.** *Constraint Translate and Rotate attributes*

A constraint was added. The reason you added this constraint to the group and not the mesh is that the mesh can be changed or adapted if needed. You also need to add constraints to the joints. In the following steps, be sure not to confuse group meshes, joints, or controls.

1.  Back in the Outliner, select ctrl_head (A1) then hold Ctrl and select jnt_head (A2) and from the top menu to choose Constrain ➤ Parent (see Figure 8-50).

2.  In the View Panel, if you select the head control curve, you can rotate the head with the Rotate tool (E).

3.  Undo the rotation movements of the head (press Ctrl+Z).

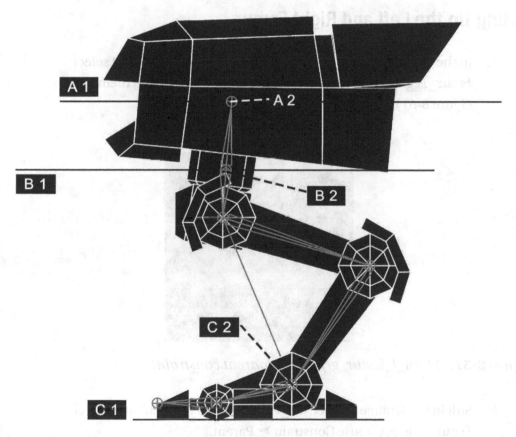

***Figure 8-50.*** *Joints and which controllers constraint them*

## Setting Up the Body Control

The body (B2) should follow the root joint (B1), as illustrated in Figure 8-51.

1. In the Outliner, first select jnt_root then hold Ctrl and select mech_body_grp. Choose Constrain ➤ Parent from the top menu.

2. Select ctrl_root then hold Ctrl and select jnt_root. Choose Constrain ➤ Parent from the top menu.

The body control should also drive the movement of the head:

3. In the correct order, select ctrl_head then ctrl_root. Then press P (to parent them).

## Setting Up the Left and Right Femur

1. In the Outliner, first select jnt_l_femur then hold Ctrl and select femur_l_grp. Choose Constrain ➤ Parent from the top menu (see Figure 8-51).

***Figure 8-51.*** *Mech_l_femur_grp with a parent constraint*

2. Still in the Outliner, select jnt_r_femur then hold Ctrl and select femur_r_grp. Choose Constrain ➤ Parent.

## Setting Up the Left and Right Tibia

1.  In the Outliner, first select jnt_l_knee then hold Ctrl and select
    mech_l_tibia_grp. Choose Constrain ➤ Parent.

2.  Still in the Outliner, select jnt_r_knee then hold Ctrl and select
    mech_r_tibia_grp. Choose Constrain ➤ Parent.

## Setting Up the Feet

To complete the following steps, you may have to expand the joints in the Outliner to
locate the ball joints:

1.  In the Outliner, select ctrl_l_foot and hold Ctrl and select
    IK_l_leg. Then, choose Constrain ➤ Parent.

2.  In the Outliner, select ctrl_l_foot and then hold Ctrl and select
    IK_r_leg. Then, choose Constrain ➤ Parent.

3.  In the Outliner, select ctrl_l_foot and then hold Ctrl and select
    jnt_l_ball. Then, choose Constrain ➤ Parent.

4.  In the Outliner, select ctrl_l_foot and hold Ctrl and select
    jnt_l_toe. Then, choose Constrain ➤ Parent.

5.  In the Outliner, select ctrl_r_foot and then hold Ctrl and select
    jnt_r_ball. Then, choose Constrain ➤ Parent.

6.  In the Outliner, select ctrl_r_foot and then hold Ctrl and select
    jnt_r_toe. Then, choose Constrain ➤ Parent.

7.  Still in the Outliner, select jnt_l_ball then hold Ctrl and select
    mech_l_foot_grp. Then, choose Constrain ➤ Parent.

8.  Select jnt_r_ball then hold Ctrl and select mech_r_foot_grp.
    Then, choose Constrain ➤ Parent.

9.  Select jnt_l_toe then hold Ctrl and select mech_l_toe_grp.
    Choose Constrain ➤ Parent.

10. Still in the Outliner, select jnt_r_toe then hold Ctrl and select
    mech_r_toe_grp. Choose Constrain ➤ Parent.

11.  Select ctrl_l_knee and hold Ctrl and select ctrl_r_knee, then
     select ctrl_root last.

12.  With the knee and main controls selected, press P (to parent
     them).

# Creating a Grouping System

For exporting purposes, you need to have everything (including the meshes, joints, and
controls) all together.

1.  In the Outliner, select all of the controls (ctrl_head, ctrl_root,
    ctrl_l_foot, ctrl_r_foot, ctrl_l_knee, and ctrl_r_knee).

2.  With all of the controls selected from the previous step, press
    Ctrl+G (to group them). Double-click this group and rename it
    ctrl_grp.

3.  Choose jnt_root and press Ctrl+G (to group it). Double-click this
    group and rename it jnt_grp.

4.  Ctrl-select IK_l_leg and IK_r_leg, then press Ctrl+G (to group it).
    Then rename it IKs_grp.

5.  Finally select char_mech_01_low, ctrl_grp, IKs_grp, and jnt_grp
    and press Ctrl+G (to group them together). Double-click this
    group and rename it mech_01.

6.  Expand the mech_01 group and rename the char_mech_01_low to
    geo_grp (see Figure 8-52).

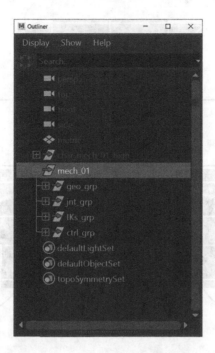

*Figure 8-52.* *Mech_01 group*

---

**Tip**   You can organize the object nodes and the order that they appear in the Outliner by clicking the middle mouse button and dragging them up or down to rearrange them.

---

You will end up with a full final mech rig that will be used in the next chapter (see Figure 8-53).

7.   Save the rig (choose File ➤ Save).

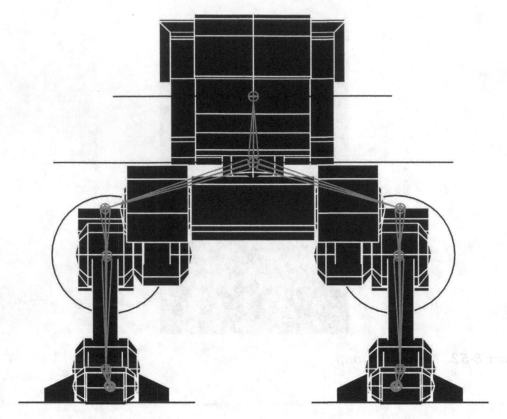

***Figure 8-53.*** *Final mech rig*

# Summary

In this chapter, you created a finished rig that can be utilized by an animator. The chapter discussed the importance of the technical animator communicating with the animator to understand the needs of the mech's movement. You also worked with joints, learning how to create, move, and mirror them. Then, you learned about control curves and created them for the body, head, knees, and feet, followed by adding inverse kinematics and vector poles. Finally, you added constraints that connected the controls to the meshes and grouped everything into an organized system.

# CHAPTER 9

# Bringing the Asset to Life

In this chapter, you finish the 3D asset pipeline with animation, texture, and material applications. The chapter covers the role of the game engine. It will recap the iterative design process, explain how to animate the mech, install Unity, and import the mech assets you have been working on throughout this book.

## Iterative Design

The book has gone through an entire asset pipeline from the block-out stage, low poly, high poly, texturing, and rigging, and now you need to animate and import the asset into a game engine. As you may recall, the game asset goes through a series of iterations after a playtest. The asset will usually make it to the game as a primitive shape for an early prototype or a basic block-out. Then, the asset will be imported without textures.

The idea is to follow the entire asset pipeline. This means that at every vertical slice, the asset is imported into the game, from a simple gray box look to the polished version. Problems with the asset on other game design elements can be spotted early on, thus saving a lot of production time. Imagine if you follow an entire asset pipeline only to find out that the asset is the incorrect size at the end. For this reason, an iterative process should be used in all aspects of creating game assets. Figure 9-1 illustrates the iterative game design process. The prototype box includes a game that might consist of an entire gameplay loop so that the player can go through the loop, win or lose. This can be as simple as using primitive shapes as placeholders for art.

© Nova Villanueva 2022
N. Villanueva, *Beginning 3D Game Assets Development Pipeline*,
https://doi.org/10.1007/978-1-4842-7196-4_9

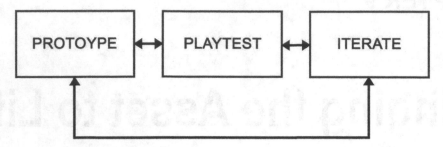

***Figure 9-1.*** *Flowchart of the iterative game design process*

**Note**    *Vertical slice* is a type of benchmark that showcases a portion of a game and the progress across all of its components as the game is meant to look in its final state.

# Animating the Mech

Although this book is read linearly, the animator's role was crucial even before starting to animate in this chapter. The animator's needs and expectations have been considered by the team since the beginning (see Figure 9-2). The concept artist and 3D artist communicate with the animator to see if the designs are appropriate for animation. Then, the technical animator makes sure that their controls for animation reach the capabilities of movements desired by the animator. To animate your mech, you need to first understand animation states. Then you will read about the Time Slider, frames, and keyframes.

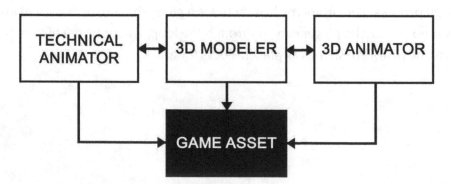

***Figure 9-2.*** *Flowchart of the role of the 3D animator as part of the pipeline*

# Animation States

A 3D asset can have different states, such as idle, walk, run, jump, and attack. Game programming will then transition the state from one to the other. Each state is usually made up of an animation that can be set to repeat over and over again or loop in the game engine. For instance, the walk cycle could be less than a second long, but with looping, a player in the game can walk for a longer amount of time. Animation states can be paired up with animation rigging, where parts of the rig can be adapted while the game is running. For example, a player's foot can be adjusted based on hilly terrain.

# Setting Up the Scene for Animation

For the following steps, you can continue with the rig you made in Chapter 8 or open the start file named start_ch9.

You will see the Time Slider (see Figure 9-3) and the Range Slider (see Figure 9-4) at the bottom of Maya. You will be using these panels to animate your mech. Refer back to Chapter 2 if you need to review what the Time Slider and Range Slider's function and purpose are.

*Figure 9-3.* *Time Slider*

*Figure 9-4.* *Range Slider*

You can set the start time of the animation or the playback range by inserting values into the two left slots of the Range Slider. Meanwhile, you can set the end time of the animation or the playback range by inserting values into the two right slots.

The Range Slider should start at 1 and end at 150 frames and display from 1-150. It should look as shown in Figure 9-4.

When you start animating, it is always important to make sure your frame rate matches the project you are trying to create. The standard frame rate is 30 frames per second, which is the industry standard at the time of writing this book. You can set this up from right side of the Range Slider. Change the dropdown menu to 30 fps (see Figure 9-5) if it is not set this way already.

*Figure 9-5. Range Slider dropdown set to 30 fps*

# Creating the Idle Animation

Let's create the idle animation by posing the mech and creating keyframes on it. Keyframes record transform data in a given location of a timeline. you can set a keyframe by selecting the object in the scene and pressing S. Depending on where you are in the Time Slider or what frame you have selected, a keyframe will be set there. To change the current frame, you can click and drag through the Time Slider or manually change the number in the current frame slot (see Figure 9-6).

*Figure 9-6. Time Slider showing frame one as the current frame selected*

## Adding Keyframes to the Mech

If you recall from Chapter 8, you only want to add keyframes to your control curves. Based on how you set your rig up, you will be able to set them back to 0 if you need to.

You can spread the feet along the Z axis so the idle state looks more natural:

1. Select `ctrl_r_foot`, press W, and translate it forward along the Z axis (see Figure 9-7).

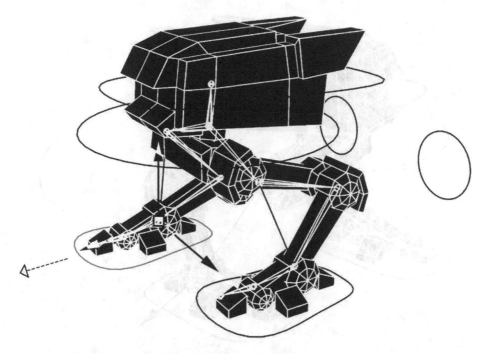

***Figure 9-7.*** *Right foot control moved forward*

2.  To set a keyframe on this foot pose, you first need to make sure you have frame 1 selected and that it is the current frame in the Time Slider.

3.  With `ctrl_r_foot` still selected, press S to set a keyframe, as shown in Figure 9-7.

The keyframe appears on the Time Slider with the creation of a vertical thin red bar on the affected frame. If you deselect the control that has the keyframe, it will not show up anymore. To see the keyframes, the object has to be selected.

4.  Select `ctrl_l_foot`, transform it backward along the Z axis, and press S to set another keyframe on frame 1 (see Figure 9-8).

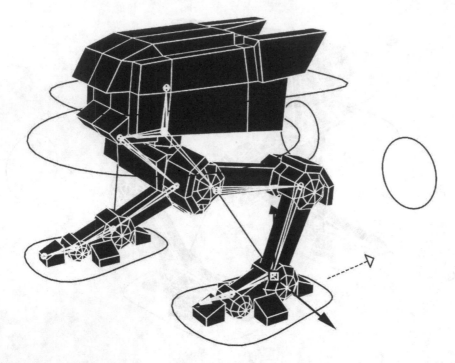

***Figure 9-8.***  *Left foot control moved backward*

There are exceptions, but a standard idle character animation for the most part is usually subtle, with the character's feet planted on the ground at all times. For this reason, let's move on and animate the body with the following steps:

1.  Still in frame 1, choose `ctrl_root` and press S to add a keyframe to it.

2.  Then, with `ctrl_root` still selected, choose frame 150 in the Time Slider and press S (see Figure 9-9).

To recap how to add a keyframe, you first select and alter the desired control curve's position, and then press S. You always press S last. If you want to change an existing frame's keyframes, it will override animations if you make changes and then press S.

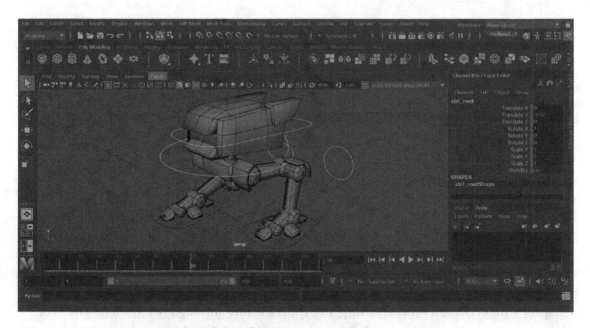

***Figure 9-9.*** *Root control with keyframes*

3.  With `ctrl_root` still selected, choose frame 80 in the Time Slider.

4.  In the Channel Box, change Translate Y to -0.02 and Rotate X to 1 of `ctrl_root`, as shown in Figure 9-10. This is supposed to be a subtle difference.

5.  Then, with `ctrl_root` still selected, press S (to add a kcyframe to it).

***Figure 9-10.*** *Channel Box showing the ctrl_root's transforms*

6.  Press the Play button (see Figure 9-11) to preview the animation.

**Figure 9-11.** *Play button*

---

**Note**   Use the Esc key to stop animation playback.

---

## Deleting Keyframes

To delete a keyframe, First, select the control curve you want to delete the keyframes on. Then, in the Time Slider, right-click the frame and choose Delete from the popup menu.

## Exporting the Animated Mech

Chapter 7 first covered FBX exporting, to export the low and high res models. The FBX file format holds information such as the asset itself, textures, and animations. Unity, our game engine for this book, can read and import this file.

You should already have the FBX extension loaded in Maya; however, refer back to Chapter 7 if you need to review how to reload it.

1.  Open the Outline if it is not already opened (choose Windows ➤ Outliner).

2.  In the Outliner, select mech_01 (see Figure 9-12).

**Figure 9-12.** *Outliner with mech_01 group selected*

3.  With mech_01 selected, choose File ➤ Export Selection from the top menu.

4. In the Export Selection window, change the dropdown menu to FBX and name the file mechAnim1 (see Figure 9-13).

**Figure 9-13.** *The Export Selection window*

5. On the right side of this window, change the settings to enable Animation and Bake Animation, as shown in Figure 9-14.

**Figure 9-14.** *Plug-in manager animation settings*

6. Find the location where you want the file to be exported to and select Export Selection. You may get a warning in this step. This can be ignored for the most part.

7. Save this file (choose File ➤ Save).

All you need for Unity is this FBX file. After you add this file to Unity, the FBX file can be altered and, as long as the name is the same, Unity will update its changes automatically. When we talked about iterative design at the beginning of this chapter, this is one of the scenarios we were referring to. Usually, you start with a simple FBX of a graybox for a character, then as production progresses, it will get updated.

# Installing and Opening Unity

Download Unity from store.unity.com/download and install it. Personal, Plus, and Pro versions are available. All the different licenses offer full features. You need to download Unity Hub first using the previous link. When you run the program the first time, you need to create a new user account. Unity 2021 was used at the time of writing this book.

If you choose to add Unity's shortcut app to your desktop on installation, you can double-click the program's icon to start it. Unity can also be opened from the Windows Start menu ➤ Program Files ➤ Unity, and on the Mac, by choosing Applications ➤ Unity.

After Unity starts, the Hub screen will open. You can create a new project, add an existing one, or open projects that have been previously opened on your computer.

# Overview of Unity

Unity is a powerful game engine used by many, from hobbyists to professionals. The role of a game engine is essentially to compile all elements that make up a game, including assets, animation, lighting, shaders, audio, physics, level design, artificial intelligence, and visual effects with computer programming. This chapter explores Unity's interface and shows you how to create a new project. You'll also learn how to navigate Unity, import the mech, and connect its animation.

# Creating a New Project

1.   In Unity's hub window, choose New (see Figure 9-15).

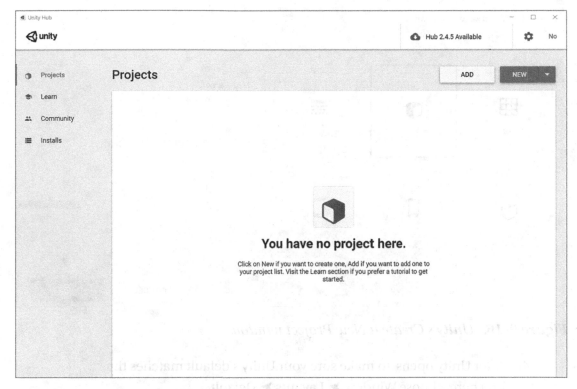

*Figure 9-15.* *Unity's hub window*

2. Give the project a name and specify a location to store the project files, as shown in Figure 9-16.

3. Select the 3D template and click Create.

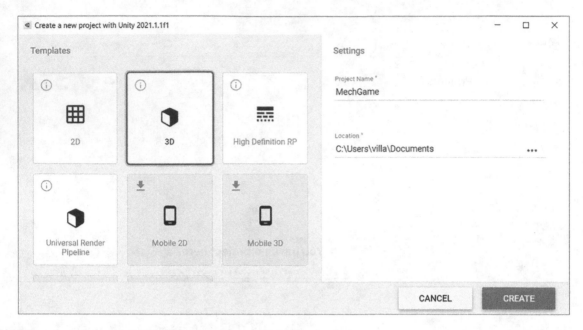

***Figure 9-16.*** *Unity's Create a New Project window*

4.  After Unity opens, to make sure your Unity's default matches the one here, choose Window ➤ Layouts ➤ Default.

## Navigating in the Scene View

The good news is that the navigation in Unity's Scene view is the same as in Maya. To recap:

- **Alt+hold the left mouse button:** To rotate around the scene.

- **Alt+hold the middle mouse button:** To pan.

- **Alt+hold the right mouse button:** To zoom in and out.

## Understanding the Interface

Unity consists of several windows that can be dragged and repositioned. The interface includes a top menu, scene view, game view, hierarchy, Inspector, and project windows (see Figure 9-17). I explain more about this as you work on your project.

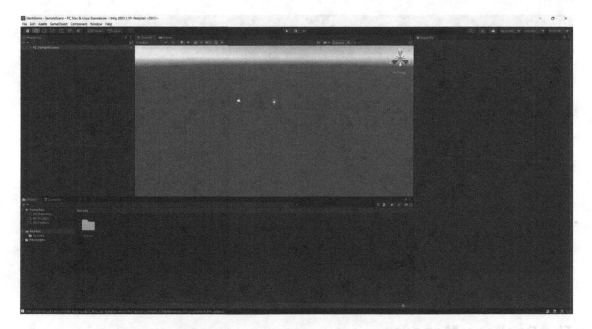

***Figure 9-17.*** *Unity's interface*

# The Project Window

The Project window (see Figure 9-18) is located toward the bottom left of the Unity window. When you create a project, Unity will create and populate an Assets folder in the location you provided in the previous step. In this root folder, you can create additional folders to organize your project. It is common to make folders for project content, such as scripts and art content. This automatically generated folder structure will help you keep an organized project from the start.

Be aware that any changes you make to this folder outside of Unity will be reflected in Unity. For instance, if you replace artwork outside of Unity, Unity will refresh to the updated artwork. You can also delete items and even restore them from your desktop's trash can. The idea is that Unity is simply working directly from the stored files on your computer; it does not create a clone of them to work with. Being this intuitive with file handling is one of the strengths of Unity.

**Figure 9-18.** *Project window*

## The Package Manager

One of the strengths of using Unity over other game engines is its powerful package manager. The idea is that unless your game needs a specific component, Unity will by default load only a lightweight project. For instance, if your game is only in 3D, there is no need to have everything that Unity has available for 2D projects in the engine. Moreover, the package manager makes it easy to update features, add them, or delete them at any time. To view this package manager, choose Window ➤ Package Manager from the top menu.

# Working with Assets in Unity

Choose Assets ➤ Import New Asset... from the top menu and locate the mechAnim1.fbx file exported in the previous section. As an alternative, you can also drag the FBX file from the computer window directly into the Unity Project window (see Figure 9-19).

The mech should now be imported into the Unity project as a model.

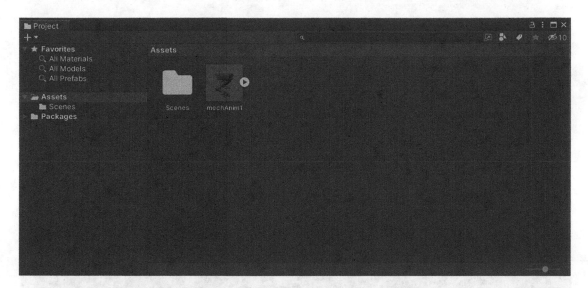

**Figure 9-19.** *Project window with the mech asset imported*

## Using the Hierarchy

The Hierarchy is in the top left and shows all the game objects that are currently in the open scene. Right now, there are two game objects in the scene—*Main Camera* and *Directional Light*. If you are missing one, you can add it from the top menu (choose GameObject ➤ Camera). You can now add the mech to the scene.

1. From the Project window, hold and select mechAnim1.fbx and drag and drop to the Hierarchy window to add the asset to the scene.

2. In the Hierarchy, choose mechAnim1.

3. With mechAnim1 selected, hover the mouse pointer on top of the Scene window and press F to frame the mech (see Figure 9-20).

***Figure 9-20.*** *Framed mech asset in the scene window*

## Using the Inspector

The Inspector located on the right side of Unity lets you make changes to game objects, including transforming them, adding components, and changing their settings. Depending on the item you selected, the Inspector will show you the settings or components attached to it.

1. In the Project window, choose `mechAnim1` for the Inspector to show the settings, as shown in Figure 9-21.

***Figure 9-21.*** *The Inspector window showing settings for mechAnim1*

2.  Select the Animation tab (see Figure 9-22).

3.  Rename the clip take from Take 001 (see Figure 9-23) to Idle (see Figure 9-24) and press Enter.

***Figure 9-22.*** *Animation tab*

***Figure 9-23.*** *Clip take name, Take 001*

***Figure 9-24.*** *Clip properties renamed to Idle*

4.    Enable Loop Time (see Figure 9-25).

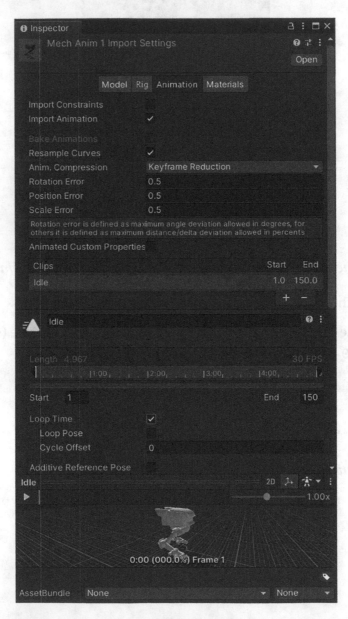

***Figure 9-25.*** *Animation tab with Loop Time enabled*

5.  Then, scroll down until you see the Apply button and click it (see Figure 9-26).

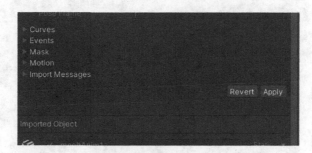

***Figure 9-26.*** *Revert or Apply buttons on the Animation tab*

6.  From the top menu, choose Assets ➤ Create ➤ Animator Controller.

This animation controller will show up at the bottom within the Project window (see Figure 9-27). This controller is used to house different animation states and its transitions from one to another. Then, with computer programming in C#, they can be called when needed in the game. You can add the idle state animation using the following steps:

***Figure 9-27.*** *Animator controller inside the project window.*

You can add the idle state animation using the following steps:

1.  In the Project window, double-click the new animator controller to open it in the Animator panel (see Figure 9-28).

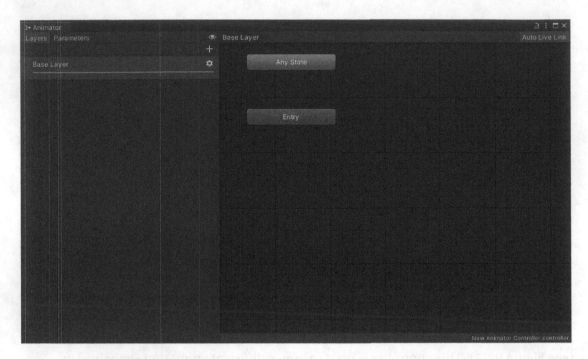

***Figure 9-28.*** *Animator panel*

2.  Back in the Project window, select the arrow 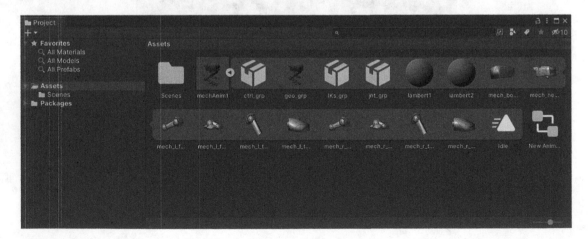 to the right of
    mechAnim1 to expand it.

Any animations in the FBX model will always show toward the end. The animation
that you named Idle is shown as a triangular icon (see Figure 9-29).

***Figure 9-29.*** *Expanded FBX file*

3. Select and drag the `Idle` animation on top of the grid area of the animator controller you previously opened (see Figure 9-30).

There is now a connection from the entry of the game to `Idle` (see Figure 9-30). You can create more animation states in Maya in the same way. Then they could be added to this same animator, such as a walk state to connect from `Idle`, where a player can transition from one to the other.

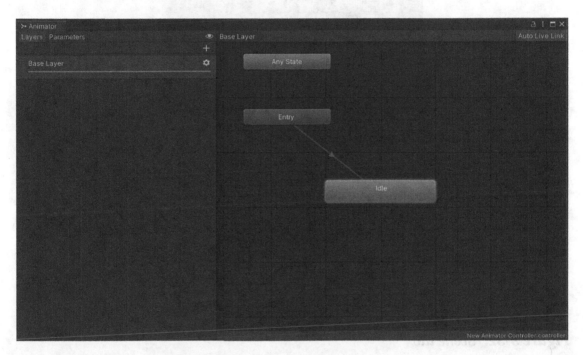

***Figure 9-30.*** *Idle animation inside the animator*

In Maya, you animated only from frames 1 to 150. You could add more frames for new states if you wanted to and Unity can crop the animation for you, as shown in Figure 9-31.

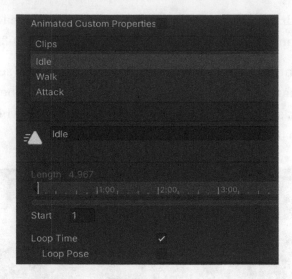

***Figure 9-31.*** *Animation settings for the asset*

4.  Select the Scene tab (see Figure 9-32) to switch out of the animator controller window.

***Figure 9-32.*** *Scene tab*

5.  Then, in the hierarchy, choose mechAnim1 (see Figure 9-33).

***Figure 9-33.*** *Hierarchy window with mechAnim1 selected*

6.  With mechAnim1 still selected, in the Inspector to the right side
    of the interface, choose Add Component (see Figure 9-34) and
    search for Animator from the dropdown menu. Select it.

***Figure 9-34.*** *The Inspector window*

An animator component should have been added to the Inspector, as shown in Figure 9-35.

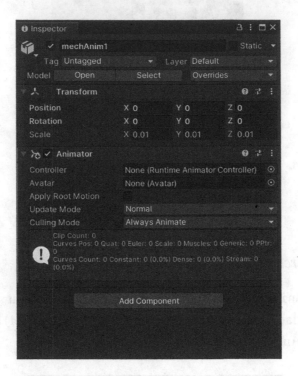

**Figure 9-35.** *Animator component added*

7.  Select the small circle to the right of None (Runtime Animator Controller) and click New Animator Controller, as shown in Figure 9-36.

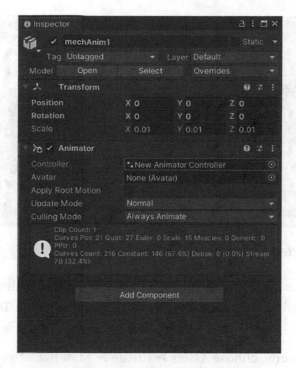

***Figure 9-36.*** *Animator controller added to the Inspector*

The asset is now connected to its idle animation.

# Adding Textures to the Mech

You need to add the textures that you created in Chapter 7 to continue bringing your mech to life.

1. In the top menu, choose Assets ➤ Import New Asset.

2. In the Import window, select the mech's textures. There are four essential textures that you need to bring in for the body and leg models: Basecolor, Roughness, Metallic, and Normal map (see Figure 9-37).

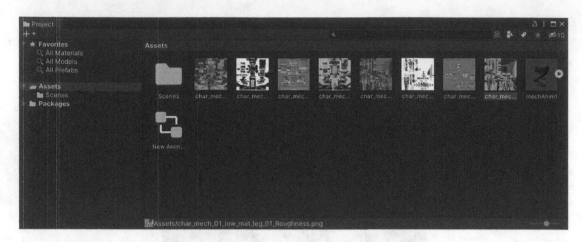

*Figure 9-37.  Imported textures*

Now that you have added the textures, let's create the two materials just like you did in Maya when setting up for texturing in Painter in Chapter 7. To do that, follow these steps:

1.  In the top menu, choose Assets ➤ Create ➤ Material.

This new material will show up at the bottom in the Project window (see Figure 9-38).

*Figure 9-38.  New material inside the Project window*

2.  Create another material from the top menu or hold and right-click within the Project window, to bring up the popup menu. Choose Create ➤ Material.

298

3.  Double-click its name to rename it mat_body (material). Double-
    click the other one and rename it mat_leg (see Figure 9-39.

By renaming them, the materials will shift places according to the alphabetical
ordering of the assets in the folder, as shown in Figure 9-39.

***Figure 9-39.*** *Rename materials for body and leg*

# Changing Shaders and Linking Textures to the Map Slots

Now you need to change the shader type of the material so that it supports all of your
PBR maps.

1.  Select the mat_body material. In the Inspector, change the Shader from Standard to Autodesk Interactive (see Figure 9-40).

*Figure 9-40. Shader set to Autodesk Interactive*

You should see the properties change so that there is now an input slot to insert the Roughness map.

Since you have all of the appropriate texture slots, you need to link the texture maps to them. Let's start with the body's *basecolor*.

1.  With the mat_body still selected, in the Project window, select and drag the body *basecolor* map into the square to the left of the Albedo input slot. The texture will appear in the square if it connects successfully (see Figure 9-41).

---

**Tip**    You can identify the texture maps by selecting them and seeing their name appear in the Inspector.

---

**Figure 9-41.** *Basecolor texture linked to the Albedo slot*

Another method of linking textures is to search for the texture map directly from the square to the left of each slot.

2.  With mat_body still selected, click the little circle to the left of the Metallic input slot.

3.  A Select Texture window will pop up.

4.  Search for metallic and select the texture containing the body label, as shown in Figure 9-42.

***Figure 9-42.*** *Metallic texture linked to the metallic slot*

Using one of the two methods discussed, connect the roughness and normal texture maps to the material.

With the mat_body still selected, you can view the completed material with all four texture maps hooked up. You do this in the material previewer at the bottom of the Inspector, as shown in Figure 9-43.

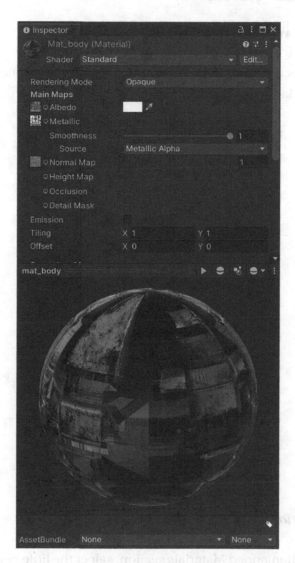

***Figure 9-43.*** *Material previewer at the bottom of the Inspector*

For the leg material, repeat the previous steps and the same process for changing shaders and linking the textures to the appropriate map slots.

# Assigning the Materials to the Mech Asset

1.  In the Project window, select mechAnim1, and in the Inspector, select the Materials tab (see Figure 9-44).

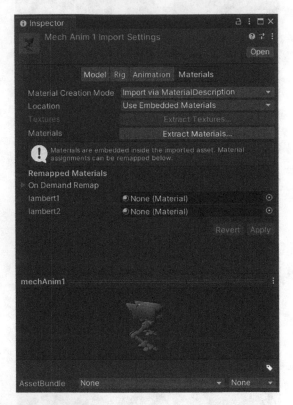

***Figure 9-44.*** *Material tab in the Inspector*

2.  Under the Remapped Materials section, select the little circle to the right of the lambert1 slot.

3.  The Select Material window will appear. Scroll down and double-click mat_leg (see Figure 9-45).

***Figure 9-45.*** *Select Material window*

4.  Select the little circle to the right of the `lambert2` slot.

5.  The Select Material window will pop up again. Choose `mat_body`.

6.  The input slots should be filled with your created materials, as shown in Figure 9-46.

7.  Click Apply.

**Figure 9-46.** *Remapped materials in the Inspector*

You should now see your mech fully textured in the Viewport (see Figure 9-47).

**Figure 9-47.** *Textured mech in Viewport*

# Working with Level of Details

Throughout the modeling and texturing creation processes, you constantly kept an eye on the balance of detail based on the factors of scale and the distance by which model would be viewed from. However, you may wonder, what if the camera that was originally far away from the model gets closer to it? Or vice versa?

It would make sense to swap it for another model with the appropriate detail, therefore that is what can happen. A lot of game engines use a system called LOD (*Level of Detail*). This is where you can feed the engine multiple poly-counted models that will change based on how far the player is from the given model. This is an efficient system that ensures only the necessary level of detail is shown on a model to help with game performance.

# Playing the Scene

Unity will let you preview the game in runtime with the click of a button. Pressing the Play button will turn it blue (see Figure 9-48). The scene window will change to the game window when in play mode and it will start a view from the Main Camera's position. To stop playing the game, click the Play button again. Be aware that any changes you make while the play mode is active are not saved by Unity.

***Figure 9-48.*** *Blue play button*

# What About Other Assets?

The asset should now be looping the animation when in play mode. This concludes the integration of the asset into Unity. All assets can be integrated the same way. Some of them will have animation and textures while others may not. Unity handles this part for you. The best way to update files in Unity is by replacing them from outside of Unity using Windows Explorer or the Finder app on a Mac. In the Project window, right-click the mechAnim1 file and select Show in Explorer from the dropdown menu (Reveal from the Finder on a Mac). The file will open where it is stored on the computer. This is the folder where you can directly save your exported update files from Maya.

# Summary

In this chapter, you finished the 3D asset pipeline with animation, texture, and material application, and understanding the role of a game engine. The chapter further discussed the iterative design process, animated the mech, and brought the asset to life in Unity.

# Wrapping It All Up

This book covered a single asset throughout its life in the development of game production. It is crucial to understand that, although this book was written linearly, with the overall knowledge obtained by going from one phase to the other, the asset pipeline is not always linear.

As shown in Figure 9-49, after any game asset is added to the game, it may continue to get iterated on. And mentioned, you'll never wait until the asset is fully polished to put it into the game. Using primitive-looking assets before the textures, rigging, and animation stages can not only save production time, but also help in finding problems early on. Then with the benefit of pipeline vertical slices, the team can integrate more and more until the asset is polished and as the industry says, "Ship it!"

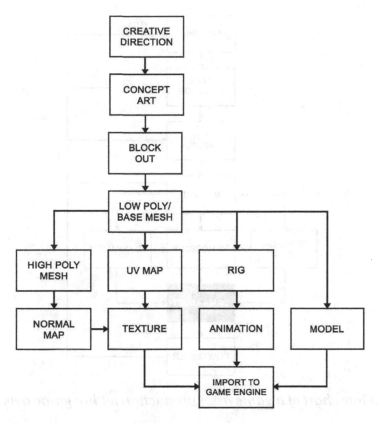

*Figure 9-49.* *Flow chart of different phases within the asset pipeline*

# Where Do You Go From Here?

As you may have noticed throughout the book, the entire asset pipeline consists of different roles that specialize in different areas in production (see Figure 9-50) and again in the industry.

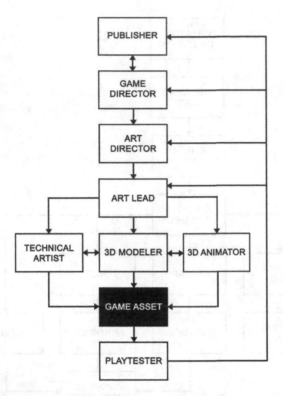

***Figure 9-50.***  *Flow chart of a game asset production within game development*

Now that you have an overall picture of the entire production and the requirements from one stage to the other, you can learn more about the different stages. The more you know about each of them, the better you will understand how it works as a whole. If you want to be a specialist in a given area, the better you will understand how you can work as a team member.

# Staying Inspired

The fundamental key to keeping the spirit, velocity, and energy alive as a game developer or 3D artist is to stay inspired! Continue to revisit what made you seek out this career path in the first place or look in new places to draw inspiration. The world is a never-ending source of inspiration, especially for a 3D artist!

# Index

## A

Animation states, 274, 275, 291, 293
Arranging/packing UVs, 138
Asset, 1, 2, 13, 308
Automatic mapping, 119, 126, 127

## B

Base mesh
  armor, motor units, 79–81
  build body, 81–83
  build head, 84, 85
  component, 55
  concave faces, 60
  definition, 56
  display modes, 72
  edge loops, 56
  exceptions, 57
  foot stabilizers, 77, 79
  head, adding thickness
    leg/body, 86
    modeling, 87–91
    neck model, 91, 92
    positioning leg, 92
  image plane reference, 62–64
  instancing leg, 93, 95
  leg connectors, 73–76
  metrics, 60, 61
  modeling, 65, 66
  panel views, switching, 64, 65

shape head, 85, 86
symmetrical editing, 67, 68, 70, 71
topology, 57, 59

## C

Constraints
  controls, 263
  creating groups
    body control, 268
    grouping system, 270, 272
    left/right femur, 268
    left/right Tibia, 269
    poly meshes, 264, 265
    setting up feet, 269
    setting up head control, 266, 267
  definition, 263
Construction history, 101, 102, 114
Construction nodes, 101
Control curves
  creating, 244–246
  editing vertices, 247, 248
  feet controls, 251, 252, 254, 255
  knee controls, 256, 258, 260
  object mode, 248, 250

## D, E

Destructive approach, 166
Duplicate Special Instance method, 93

311

© Nova Villanueva 2022
N. Villanueva, *Beginning 3D Game Assets Development Pipeline*,
https://doi.org/10.1007/978-1-4842-7196-4

# X, Y, Z

Printed in the United States
by Baker & Taylor Publisher Services

Printed in the United States
by Baker & Taylor Publisher Services